THE FIGHTER'S KITCHEN

CHRIS ALGIERI

ALPHA

Publisher Mike Sanders
Editor Christopher Stolle
Senior Designer Jessica Lee
Art Director William Thomas
Photographer Kelley Jordan Schuyler
Food Stylist Savannah Norris
Proofreader Lisa Starnes
Indexer Brad Herriman

First American Edition, 2019
Published in the United States by DK Publishing
6081 E. 82nd Street, Indianapolis, Indiana 46250

A catalog record for this book
is available from the Library of Congress.
ISBN 978-1-4654-8373-7
Library of Congress Catalog Number: 2018960705

DK books are available at special discounts when purchased in bulk for sales
promotions, premiums, fundraising, or educational use. For details, contact:
DK Publishing Special Markets, 1450 Broadway, Suite 801, New York, NY 10018
SpecialSales@dk.com

Printed and bound in China

All images © Dorling Kindersley Limited
For further information see: www.dkimages.com

A WORLD OF IDEAS:
SEE ALL THERE IS TO KNOW

www.dk.com

CONTENTS

SALADS & SIDES **92**

SANDWICHES & SNACKS **118**

SMOOTHIES, SHAKES & DESSERTS . . **138**

INDEX **156**

ABOUT THE AUTHOR / ACKNOWLEDGMENTS **160**

INTRODUCTION

My interest in nutrition came from my years of competitive combat sports and needing to make weight for the majority of my life. I've been ultracompetitive since an early age and I've always wanted to possess every advantage possible when it comes to game time or fight time. Performance nutrition was the route I took to maximize my potential and give me an edge over my competition.

Ever since my tortured days of high school wrestling and making weight, I knew there had to be a better way to diet and train. This eventually led to my studying nutrition and how it applies to health, fitness, and human performance. I spent countless hours researching how nutrition can affect the way we look, feel, and perform.

My affinity for food and cooking began long before my entrance into competitive fighting. I come from two cultures—Italian and Argentinean—that have deep-rooted traditions of culinary mastery. I spent many afternoons and weekends around my grandparents, learning the fine art of cooking and preparing delicious cuisine.

This book is a marriage of science and art—from my studies and experiences to my innate passion for food, fitness, and performance. Not only are these recipes healthy and nutritious, but they're also tried and true. I've been using these recipes throughout my fighting career and they've aided me in accomplishing my competitive and personal goals.

I wrote this book for all the people who have struggled to cook healthy meals for themselves in order to change their lifestyle. Performance isn't just for world-class competitive athletes. We all have to perform each day of our lives in whatever manner we choose to make our living. I approach life like I approach a bout: It's a competition—and I want to win. Whether you're an attorney in a courtroom, an accountant working in an office, or a weekend warrior triathlete, how you perform matters.

This book is meant for those who want to feel good, have tons of energy, and be mentally focused to wake up ready to attack their day. I don't care how driven you are—if you don't feel good, motivation will be lacking. Wake up with vigor and be ready to achieve your goals. The recipes that follow can help you with your objectives—even if and especially if you never compete in a cage or a ring. I hope you enjoy making and eating these meals. They're personal to me and I hope they can become personal to you. Buon appetito!

Chris Algieri

THE SCIENCE OF NUTRITION

Creating meals can feel like art, but how our bodies process foods is a science. Whether you're trying to eat better, you're a weekend warrior, or you're wanting to train to become a professional fighter—or you're somewhere in between—this chapter explains how the macronutrients you digest can help you sculpt your warrior physique.

NUTRITION BASICS

No matter your livelihood, having a warrior's mindset and a competitor's attitude can help you take on any challenge you face. How you prepare to achieve mental and physical goals—even if you never jump into the cage or the ring—is essential to success. But your training to look and feel like a fighter actually begins in the kitchen.

ENERGY

Every time you sit down at a table is a chance to improve how your body looks and feels. Every meal can potentially make you stronger and fitter, but without the proper nutritional balance, eating might make you feel slower and weaker. Developing a routine of meal frequency can help you make eating behavior changes as well as curb and control your appetite and cravings. Infrequent eating patterns can lead to sluggishness and difficulty in losing body fat. Your energy demands when working out are extremely high, and if you want to lose weight, finding the correct energy balance is key.

Small meals every 2 to 3 hours has been shown to be most effective for keeping sustained energy levels while also burning fat for fuel. Because time constraints can make eating large meals difficult, knowing what and when to eat can help ensure you get enough calories and macronutrients on any given day. Subsequent pages in this chapter discuss macronutrients and caloric needs as well as how the recipes in this book—put into weekly meal plans— can help you meet your dietary and fitness goals.

METABOLISM

Metabolism is the process by which your body breaks down the foods you eat into energy. Any excess energy is stored in fat reserves for later use. This energy balance is directly connected to how active you are in relation to how much food you eat. If you burn more calories than you consume, then you'll lose weight. (Conversely, if you consume more calories than you burn, you'll gain weight.) When your metabolism is high, your body is efficient at breaking down food and using it for cellular processes. A high metabolism breaks down fat stores to help you maintain a steady energy source.

When you're working out, your metabolic demands are different when compared with times of inactivity. When you're exercising, you're moving continuously and constantly, seamlessly switching from one energy system to another. This makes it critical for you during these high-intensity interval training (HIIT) sessions to have properly fueled your body.

Your metabolism level depends on a number of factors, including age, genetics, activity level, and diet. The first two factors are out of your control. The last two, though, are highly variable, but you can manipulate them to increase your body's fat-burning potential. High metabolism equals high fat-burning efficiency, leading to lean muscle mass and increased energy—and a readiness to work toward reaching your personal and professional goals.

NUTRITION ESSENTIALS

Macronutrients have that name for a reason: They're the top-level building blocks you need for essential body processes. Without proper nutrition, all the physical movement in the world won't help you overcome a calorie surplus. Thus, frequently eating nutrient-rich foods throughout the day is key to a healthy and vigorous lifestyle, especially meals that combine healthy fats, nutritious carbohydrates, and lean proteins.

FATS

WHAT ARE THEY?

Despite their name, fats are actually nutrients your body needs for many different processes. Although there are bad fats, there are also good fats that your body needs and uses.

WHAT DO THEY DO?

Fats have many different functions in your body:

- Storing energy
- Absorbing vitamins and minerals
- Building cell membranes
- Clotting blood
- Moving muscles
- Fighting inflammation

Fats supply essential fatty acids and fat-soluble vitamins that are important to your diet. Consume more heart-healthy and anti-inflammatory fats (poly- and monounsaturated fats) rather than trans fats and saturated fats (although the latter fats aren't always bad).

WHAT FOODS HAVE THEM?

Animal products, nuts, oils, certain fish, and dairy are good sources of fat. Avocados, dark chocolate, and chia seeds have high fat amounts, but they also have various health benefits.

HYDRATION

Making hydration an ongoing daily routine is vital for success with your fitness goals. You can eat right and exercise right, but if you're not replacing lost fluids, you're not giving your body the best chance to become healthier and fitter. Hydration is important for every cellular process as well as proper metabolism and the absorption of nutrients.

Dehydration has several significant mental and physical consequences:

- Raises your body temperature
- Makes your body work harder at lower exercise intensities

CARBOHYDRATES

WHAT ARE THEY?

Carbs are critical nutrient sources for your body. They're classified as simple (such as honey) and complex. Complex carbs are further broken down into starches (like pasta) and dietary fiber (like fruits and vegetables).

WHAT DO THEY DO?

If you're training—and eating—to look like an MMA fighter or a boxer, carbs help you in several ways:

- Providing energy for most physical activity, including exercise
- Maintaining body mass
- Maintaining and replenishing muscle and liver glycogen stores

You can store extra carbs to use when you're lacking in carb intake or energy. Eating carbs that have many nutrients will allow you to benefit the most from them. Not getting enough carbs every day can cause headaches, fatigue, decreased mental acuity, nausea, and vitamin and mineral deficiencies.

WHAT FOODS HAVE THEM?

Grains, starchy vegetables, fruits, juices, sweets, oatmeal, and brown rice as well as whole-wheat breads, pastas, tortillas, and cereals are good sources of carbohydrates.

PROTEINS

WHAT ARE THEY?

Proteins are large molecules with one or more long chains of amino acids. They're everywhere throughout your body—from your muscles, collagen, and hair to enzymes and antibodies.

WHAT DO THEY DO?

What don't they do? Among other things, proteins do these for your body:

- Providing cell structures
- Increasing or maintaining lean muscle mass
- Helping with losing fat
- Helping with recovery after activity
- Strengthening your immune system

Simply put, your body depends on proteins. When you eat recommended protein amounts each day, you help your body survive and thrive.

WHAT FOODS HAVE THEM?

Meats, fish, dairy, eggs, whey, nuts, and legumes are good sources of protein. Specific choices include canned tuna or salmon (packed in water), eggs or egg whites, beans (pinto, black, kidney), skinless chicken breasts, lean ground beef or turkey (92 to 96% lean), top round roasts or flank steaks, turkey breasts, yogurt, string cheese, and cottage cheese.

- Causes headaches, dizziness, and fatigue
- Leads to muscle cramping and increases the risk of injury

You can monitor your hydration levels in several different ways:

- Having a clear to pale yellow urine color and needing to urinate frequently signal adequate hydration levels.
- Infrequent dark urine reflects dehydration. It might take several hours or days to recover.
- Weighing yourself before and after practice allows you to estimate fluids lost in sweat. Replace each pound lost with 3 cups of fluids

One great way to ensure you stay hydrated is to carry a refillable water bottle with you throughout the day. The longer you work out, the more you should drink. But drinking consistently throughout your day will keep you constantly properly hydrated.

And what to drink? Because our bodies are 60 to 70% water, drinking water quickly replaces lost fluids and allows your body to keep its functions going at optimal efficiency. You can always add a squirt of freshly squeezed lemon, lime, or orange juice for a little flavor. Sugary drinks and, of course, alcohol aren't going to help with recovery, but milk, juice, and coffee can help replenish lost fluids.

NUTRITION ROUTINES

Adhering to a specific eating regimen can help you focus on and reach your nutrition goals. If you have an active lifestyle, what and when you eat can have a greater impact on your physical fitness—even if you have no desire to become a fighter. Being consistent with your dietary routines is as critical for success as being consistent with your fitness routines.

USING THE RECIPES

Each recipe in this book includes the total number of calories for that meal. Many recipes offer prep tips and variations, but remember to factor in ingredient adjustments or additions to the nutrition information. All the recipes have a bar scale for the amounts of macronutrients contained in each recipe:

- One color bar means the macronutrient content is low.
- Two color bars means the macronutrient content is moderate.
- Three color bars means the macronutrient content is high.

	FAT	CARBS	PROTEIN
HIGH	15g and up	25g and up	25g and up
MEDIUM	5.1g to 14.9g	10.1g to 24.9g	10.1g to 24.9g
LOW	5g or less	10g or less	10g or less

Nutritional data for each recipe helps you see how a meal might impact you.

This dish explodes with an incredible amount of fiber and micronutrients. You can make this vegan, vegetarian, or traditional omnivorous based on what you choose to add or take away. I love this meal because there are endless combinations for making a delicious and nutritious meal.

BUDDHA BOWL
WITH RED PEPPER DRESSING

Makes 3 servings | Serving size 1 bowl | Prep time 5 minutes | Cook time 10 minutes

NUTRITION FACTS
per serving

CALORIES
315

TOTAL FAT
7 g

TOTAL CARBS
32 g

PROTEIN
33 g

INGREDIENTS

1 cup chickpeas
1 tsp extra virgin olive oil
½ tsp smoked paprika
½ tsp turmeric
½ tsp chili powder
½ tsp salt
1 portobello mushroom cap, sliced
6 cherry tomatoes, halved
1½ cups bean sprouts
1 cup cooked quinoa
3 cups mixed greens

1 medium avocado, sliced
½ cup edamame
1 tbsp sesame seeds

for the dressing
12oz (340g) roasted red peppers
1 tbsp extra virgin olive oil
juice of ½ lemon
2 garlic cloves
1 tsp sea salt
1 tsp ground black pepper

DIRECTIONS

1 Preheat the oven to 425°F (218°C).

2 In a bowl, combine the chickpeas, olive oil, paprika, turmeric, chili powder, and salt, gently tossing to evenly coat the chickpeas. Place the mixture on a baking pan lined with parchment paper. Bake until golden, about 20 to 30 minutes. Remove the chickpeas from the oven and set aside to cool.

3 In a blender on high speed, make the dressing by blending the peppers, olive oil, lemon juice, garlic, salt, and pepper until smooth. Taste and adjust the seasonings as needed. Set aside or refrigerate until needed.

4 In a saucepan on the stovetop over medium heat, cook the mushroom and tomatoes until soft and slightly browned, about 3 to 4 minutes. Add the bean sprouts and cook for 1 minute more. Remove the vegetables from the stovetop and allow to cool slightly.

5 Place equal amounts of chickpeas, quinoa, mixed greens, avocado, edamame, mushroom, and tomatoes in 3 bowls. Drizzle the red pepper dressing and sprinkle the sesame seeds over the top. Serve immediately.

PICK YOUR PLAN

Calorie recommendations and macronutrient distributions in the 7-day meal plans on the following pages can help you fuel and maximize your performance—whether you want to eat better, you want to get into better shape, or you want to train for any kind of competition. While not everyone needs the same amount of calories, you can easily adjust these plans by adhering to the same weekly adjustments (calories up or down by 500 to 1,000 per day) and keeping the macronutrient ratios the same. Each weekly meal plan includes three meals and two to three snacks per day and features recipes from this book. You can choose from four different meal plans:

MAINTENANCE MEAL PLAN

If you're happy with your weight and your body composition and want to keep your current shape and activity level, this meal plan is for you. Whether you're training to look like a fighter or you're working out to feel physically fit, this plan will help you maintain how you look and feel. It will also provide balanced types of fuel for strength and cardiovascular training.

The daily breakdown for this meal plan:
- **CALORIES:** 2,000
- **CARBS:** 50%
- **PROTEIN:** 25%
- **FAT:** 25%

STRENGTH MEAL PLAN

Protein, fat, and calories get a boost in this plan, which helps promote muscle protein synthesis. Protein sources are filled with essential amino acids and are spread out throughout each day to help promote muscle building. Carbs drop to 40% of the total calories to make room for more protein and fat—the latter acting as the predominant fuel source for lower-intensity exercise.

The daily breakdown for this meal plan:
- **CALORIES:** 2,500
- **CARBS:** 40%
- **PROTEIN:** 30%
- **FAT:** 30%

MUSCULAR ENDURANCE MEAL PLAN

This plan keeps your protein intake high and increases your calorie and carb levels to help promote aerobic and anaerobic energy production. This type of fueling will help you achieve max reps if you're weight training. Because carbs are your main source of energy for long-duration or high-intensity activities, it's important to get the majority of your total calories from carb-rich sources.

The daily breakdown for this meal plan:
- **CALORIES:** 3,000
- **CARBS:** 45%
- **PROTEIN:** 30%
- **FAT:** 25%

POWER & EXPLOSION MEAL PLAN

This meal plan offers lower-calorie intakes, with a few extra carbs throughout the day to help fuel your body during extra-explosive workouts that might be shorter than your typical workouts. Fast bursts of energy rely more heavily on carbs for fuel—and this plan will help you with those energy needs.

The daily breakdown for this meal plan:
CALORIES: 2,500
CARBS: 50%
PROTEIN: 25%
FAT: 25%

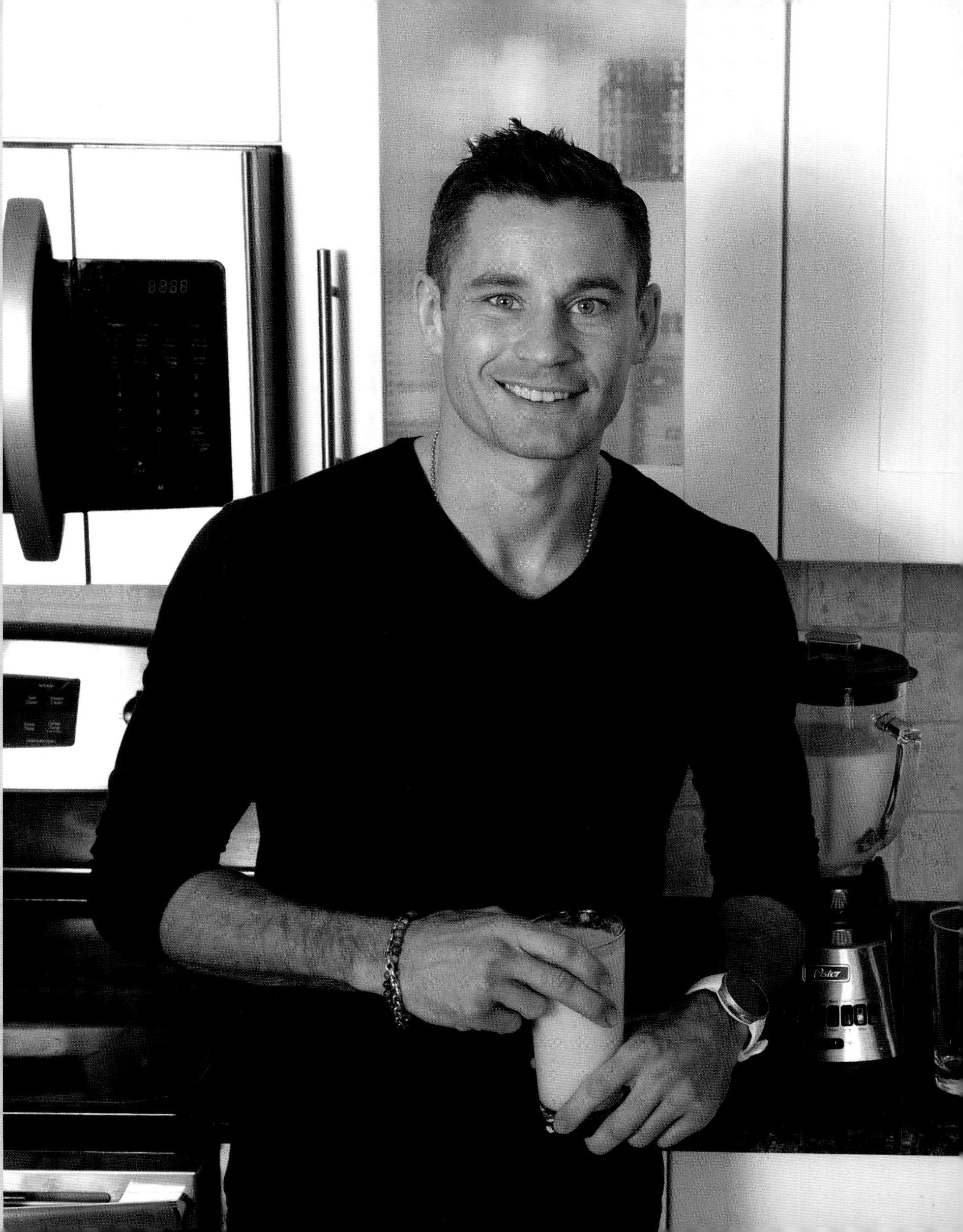

<<continued

2

COUNT YOUR CALORIES

Servings sizes in this book are for a moderately active person who weighs 160 pounds. Use these calculations to adjust the recipes to meet your daily caloric needs:

LIGHTLY ACTIVE: your weight x 12
MODERATELY ACTIVE: your weight x 13
VERY ACTIVE: your weight x 14

To stay above your basal metabolic rate—which denotes the number of calories you need for basic body functions—you should never allow your daily caloric intake to drop below 70% of your daily caloric needs.

3

PREPARE YOUR MEALS

Once you choose a meal plan, carefully review the recipes in that plan and prepare a shopping list of ingredients you need. Not only does this help you know what you need to buy, but it also helps you become familiar with the recipes and what you need to do to make each meal.

Most recipes in this book are best eaten immediately after making them, but you can easily prepare many meals in advance, portion them out, and refrigerate or freeze them until needed. This will give you more time during the week for working out, spending time with family and friends, and enjoying your favorite activities.

4

TRACK YOUR PROGRESS

Stick to your chosen meal plan for at least two weeks. Are you seeing and feeling changes in your physique and in your energy levels? Take progress pictures twice a week to help you compare and assess body composition changes. Also make sure to take a daily mental assessment to help you stay focused on what you're trying to achieve.

You don't have to do anything fancy to track your progress, but there are an endless number of apps for your phone that can allow you to track what you eat, how much you exercise, and how many calories and macronutrients you've consumed.

5

MAKE ADJUSTMENTS

If you're not gaining enough muscle mass, increase your protein intake. If you're not burning enough fat, slightly decrease the number of calories you consume each day. If you're constantly hungry, slightly increase your protein intake with each meal. Each plan comes with small snacks to help combat cravings while not having a major impact on calories or macronutrients.

But you can also swap out recipes that are nearly equal in calories and macronutrient numbers. Your most important objective is to stay flexible and make minor adjustments along the way.

THE SCIENCE OF NUTRITION

MAINTENANCE MEAL PLAN

	DAY 1	DAY 2	DAY 3
BREAKFAST	Lean 'n' Mean Turkey & Spinach Omelet Black & Blue Shake	Omega-3 Steel-Cut Oats 1 medium apple	Italian Omelet 6oz (170g) nonfat flavored Greek yogurt
SNACKS	2 medium bananas	1 medium banana	Dark Chocolate & Cherry Bars
LUNCH	California Fish Tacos Island Fruit Smoothie	Buddha Bowl 6oz (170g) grilled chicken	Turkey Burger Habenero Coleslaw
SNACKS	Homemade Hummus 15 baby carrots	Homemade Cherry & Almond Granola 15 baby carrots	1 cup nonfat cottage cheese 2 cups chopped pineapple
DINNER	Sesame-Crusted Tuna Steak Garlic & Rosemary Roasted Potatoes	Miso-Glazed Cod Ancient Grains Salad	Bison Bolognese Rice Pudding
TOTAL CALORIES	2,115	2,110	2,196
TOTAL FAT (grams)	65g	66g	62g
TOTAL CARBS (grams)	261g	241g	264g
TOTAL PROTEIN (grams)	134g	142g	144g

DAY 4	DAY 5	DAY 6	DAY 7
New York Bagel "All the Way" 1 medium mango	Mike's Dirty Waffles 2 cups chopped pineapple	Avocado & Sweet Potato Hash Spicy Carrot Juice	The Egg's Nest Homemade Cherry & Almond Granola
Dark Chocolate & Cherry Bars	Nutty Banana & Oat Bars	Nutty Banana & Oat Bars	6oz (170g) nonfat flavored Greek yogurt 1 medium banana
Balsamic-Glazed Fig & Arugula Pizza 6oz (170g) nonfat Greek yogurt	Slow-Cooked Shredded Chicken 1 whole-wheat roll 2 cups tomato soup	Southwest Steak & Corn Burrito 1 medium apple	Summertime Kale Salad 6oz (170g) grilled chicken
1 medium orange	6oz (170g) nonfat flavored Greek yogurt	6oz (170g) nonfat Greek yogurt 1 medium orange	Spicy Carrot Juice 1 medium apple
Slow-Cooked Shredded Chicken Yucca Fries 2 cups steamed broccoli	Panko-Crusted Baked Cod Broccolini & Pine Nuts 1½ cups cooked brown rice	Grilled Chicken Gyro Matcha Cooler	Oven-Roasted Flounder Mashed Sweet Potatoes
1,905	1,965	2,060	2,035
56g	61g	64g	64g
246g	238g	282g	238g
121g	128g	124g	136g

STRENGTH MEAL PLAN

	DAY 1	DAY 2	DAY 3
BREAKFAST	Knockout Keto Egg Cups Protein Pancake	The Kevo 2 cups cooked oatmeal	The Heavyweight
SNACKS	Beet Down Shake	The Counselor 2 hard-boiled eggs	6oz (170g) nonfat Greek yogurt 1 medium banana
LUNCH	Tobin's Seared Tuna Wrap Mean Green Jalapeño Smoothie	Bison Sliders Greek Salad 1 medium banana	Bison Sloppy Joes 2 cups steamed broccoli
SNACKS	Peanut Butter & Apple Crisp	Green Detox Juice 3oz (85g) roasted turkey	Frozen Greek Yogurt 1 medium mango
DINNER	Mediterranean-Style Chicken Smashed Peas & Feta	Perfectly Broiled Salmon Grilled Balsamic Asparagus Chia Protein Pudding	6oz (170g) grilled chicken Teriyaki Tofu Stir-Fry (2 servings)
TOTAL CALORIES	2,505	2,490	2,245
TOTAL FAT (grams)	89g	78g	81g
TOTAL CARBS (grams)	262g	246g	227g
TOTAL PROTEIN (grams)	183g	175g	183g

DAY 4	DAY 5	DAY 6	DAY 7
Spicy Chorizo Scramble 2 slices whole-wheat bread	The New Yorker Layered Yogurt Parfait	Avocado Toast Black & Blue Shake	5 egg whites, cooked any style Sweet Potato Hotcakes 2 slices Canadian bacon
6oz (170g) nonfat flavored Greek yogurt	Peanut Butter & Apple Crisp 3oz (85g) roasted turkey	2 hard-boiled eggs 3oz (85g) chunk light tuna in water (drained)	Peanut Butter & Apple Crisp
6oz (170g) grilled chicken 1 cup cooked quinoa 2 cups steamed green beans	Perfectly Broiled Salmon Perfect Penne	Spicy Turkey Chili Broccoli & Chickpea Salad	Open-Faced Tuna Melt 1 cup nonfat cottage cheese 2 cups chopped pineapple
Rice Cake Madness	Green Detox Juice Oatmeal & Pumpkin Seed Bars	Frozen Greek Yogurt 2 cups strawberries	Chili-Dusted Popcorn The Counselor
6oz (170g) grilled flank steak Cauliflower Mash Big Pink Smoothie	Baked Stuffed Peppers Beet Down Shake	6oz (170g) grilled chicken Turmeric-Dusted Cauliflower 1½ cups cooked brown rice	BBQ Ground Turkey (2 servings) Charred Broccoli
2,557	2,545	2,505	2,441
93g	101g	86g	87g
231g	256g	249g	246g
191g	172g	191g	167g

MUSCULAR ENDURANCE MEAL PLAN

	DAY 1	DAY 2	DAY 3
BREAKFAST	Pumpkin & Chia Overnight Oats Dark Chocolate & Cherry Bars	The Spartan 2 cups cooked oatmeal	Eggs Benedict 1 medium banana The Counselor
SNACKS	Mean Green Jalapeño Smoothie 3oz (85g) roasted turkey	1 cup nonfat cottage cheese 2 cups chopped pineapple	6oz (170g) nonfat Greek yogurt 2 medium oranges
LUNCH	Heirloom Tomato & Avocado Flatbread 6oz (170g) grilled chicken ½ cup raisins	Morning Glory Pizza 6oz (170g) chunk light tuna in water (drained)	Italian Turkey Meatballs 2 slices whole-wheat bread Island Fruit Smoothie
SNACKS	6oz (170g) nonfat Greek yogurt 1 medium banana	Avocado Twist Tuna Salad The Counselor	6oz (170g) grilled chicken Homemade Hummus
DINNER	Rosemary Roasted Chicken Garlicky Butternut Squash Big Pink Smoothie	Curried Coconut Shrimp (2 servings) 1½ cups cooked brown rice Beet Down Shake	Argentinean-Style Flank Steak 2 cups cooked quinoa 2 cups steamed broccoli
TOTAL CALORIES	2,920	2,836	3,005
TOTAL FAT (grams)	97g	83g	95g
TOTAL CARBS (grams)	334g	306g	351g
TOTAL PROTEIN (grams)	207g	202g	200g

DAY 4	DAY 5	DAY 6	DAY 7
Homemade Cherry & Almond Granola 5 egg whites, cooked any style	Layered Yogurt Parfait Green Detox Juice 1 medium banana	La Española 6oz (170g) nonfat Greek yogurt 1 medium banana	Keto Egg & Avocado Boats Island Fruit Smoothie
Spicy Carrot Juice 1 cup nonfat cottage cheese	1 medium apple 4oz (110g) roasted turkey	Oatmeal & Pumpkin Seed Bars 6oz (170g) nonfat flavored Greek yogurt	Oatmeal & Pumpkin Seed Bars ½ cup raisins
CA Turkey Cobb Salad 2 slices whole-wheat bread	Sardine Crostini 1 medium mango	Turkey Burger Spicy Zoodles 2 cups chopped pineapple	6oz (170g) grilled chicken 1 large baked sweet potato 1 medium banana
Black & Blue Shake 6oz (170g) grilled chicken	Greene Machine Smoothie 3oz (85g) chunk light tuna in water (drained)	1½ cups nonfat cottage cheese 2 cups chopped pineapple	Chia Protein Pudding 6oz (170g) chunk light tuna in water (drained)
Champ Camp Burger 1½ cups cooked brown rice Frozen Greek Yogurt ¼ cup raisins	Broiled Lamb 1½ cups cooked brown rice Beet Down Shake	Mushroom & Onion—Slathered Skirt Steak 2 cups steamed green beans 1 cup cooked quinoa Black & Blue Shake	Guinness-Braised Short Rib Stew Low-Carb Spaghetti Squash 1 medium pear
3,093	3,145	2,933	2,750
94g	88g	81g	86g
349g	351g	341g	296g
209g	225g	199g	210g

POWER & EXPLOSION MEAL PLAN

	DAY 1	DAY 2	DAY 3
BREAKFAST	Aussie Garden & Herb Scrambled Omelet 2 cups cooked oatmeal	Omega-3 Steel-Cut Oats 1 medium apple 5 egg whites, cooked any style	Protein Pancake 1 medium pear
SNACKS	Big Pink Smoothie	10 whole-grain crackers 6oz (170g) chunk light tuna in water (drained)	6oz (170g) nonfat flavored Greek yogurt 1 medium banana
LUNCH	Grilled Chicken Gyro Island Fruit Smoothie	Ancient Grains Salad Spicy Carrot Juice	Summertime Kale Salad 6oz (170g) grilled chicken ½ cup raisins
SNACKS	10 whole-grain crackers 2 medium bananas	Black & Blue Shake	Rice Cake Madness
DINNER	6oz (170g) grilled chicken Greek Salad	Crispy Red Snapper Garlic & Rosemary Roasted Potatoes 6oz (170g) nonfat flavored Greek yogurt ½ cup raisins	Perfectly Broiled Salmon Mashed Sweet Potatoes Green Detox Juice
TOTAL CALORIES	2,570	2,635	2,510
TOTAL FAT (grams)	72g	84g	68g
TOTAL CARBS (grams)	314g	343g	302g
TOTAL PROTEIN (grams)	149g	169g	169g

DAY 4	DAY 5	DAY 6	DAY 7
Southwest Steak & Corn Burrito Island Fruit Smoothie	Pumpkin & Chia Overnight Oats 1 medium banana	Mike's Dirty Waffles 2 cups chopped pineapple	The Egg's Nest Oatmeal & Pumpkin Seed Bars
New York Bagel "All the Way" 1 medium apple	Homemade Cherry & Almond Granola 6oz (170g) nonfat flavored Greek yogurt	Dark Chocolate & Cherry Bars 1 tbsp peanut butter	Peanut Butter & Apple Crisp Green Detox Juice
6oz (170g) cooked tilapia or cod Grandpa's Tomato & Cucumber Salad	Buddha Bowl 6oz (170g) grilled chicken	Perfectly Poached Egg Baked Stuffed Peppers Rice Pudding	Slow-Cooked Shredded Chicken Garlicky Butternut Squash 2 cups steamed green beans
Frozen Greek Yogurt 2 cups strawberries	Dark Chocolate & Cherry Bars	Spicy Carrot Juice 1 cup nonfat cottage cheese	Chili-Dusted Popcorn 1 medium mango
6oz (170g) grilled chicken 1½ cups cooked brown rice Spicy Zoodles	6oz grilled flank steak 1½ cups cooked brown rice Balsamic-Glazed Brussels Sprouts	Slow-Cooked Shredded Chicken Yucca Fries 2 cups steamed broccoli	Mediterranean-Style Chicken Greek Salad Chia Protein Pudding
2,495	2,630	2,593	2,675
69g	73g	84g	78g
309g	300g	307g	307g
169g	197g	168g	173g

BREAKFASTS

It's not an exaggeration that breakfast is the most important meal of the day. It's what gives you energy to start your day—whether you're on your way to work or to the gym—and what keeps you fueled until your next meal. These breakfasts have a strong mix of macronutrients, giving your body plenty of what it needs.

Colorful and light, this omelet satisfies and energizes without making you feel too full. This low-carb option is loaded with nutrients and makes for a great start to a light training day or helps you lose some extra weight. I love this on my off days because I know I won't need a lot of carbs.

NUTRITION FACTS

per serving

CALORIES

300

TOTAL FAT

24 g

TOTAL CARBS

2 g

PROTEIN

22 g

ITALIAN OMELET

| Makes | 1 serving | Serving size | 1 omelet | Prep time | 10 minutes | Cook time | 10 minutes |

INGREDIENTS

1 tbsp extra virgin olive oil

2 tsp chopped garlic

¼ cup diced summer squash

¼ cup diced zucchini

¼ cup diced tomatoes

2 tsp chopped fresh basil

2 large eggs

2 large eggs, whites only

sea salt and freshly ground black pepper

2 tsp chopped fresh parsley

DIRECTIONS

1 In a nonstick skillet on the stovetop over medium-high heat, heat the olive oil until shimmering. Add the garlic, squash, and zucchini. Cook until lightly browned and soft, about 2 minutes, stirring frequently. Add the tomatoes and basil and cook for 1 minute more. Transfer the vegetables to a bowl and set aside.

2 In a separate bowl, whisk together the eggs and egg whites and season with salt and pepper. Spray the skillet with nonstick cooking spray and return the skillet to the stovetop over medium-high heat. Quickly pour the egg mixture into the skillet. While sliding the skillet back and forth rapidly over the heat, quickly stir the eggs with a spatula to spread them continuously over the bottom of the skillet as they thicken. Cook until the eggs are firm, about 2 to 3 minutes.

3 Place the vegetables over half the omelet and fold the other half over the vegetables. Gently transfer the omelet to a plate, sprinkle the parsley over the top, and serve immediately.

CHANGE IT UP
Add feta or goat cheese for extra creaminess.

LEAN 'N' MEAN TURKEY & SPINACH OMELET

Makes *1 serving* | Serving size *1 omelet* | Prep time *5 minutes* | Cook time *10 minutes*

INGREDIENTS

½ cup egg whites

3oz (85g) low-sodium turkey breast

½ cup baby spinach

½ medium avocado, sliced

DIRECTIONS

1 Spray a skillet with nonstick cooking spray. Place the skillet on the stovetop over medium-high heat. Quickly pour the egg whites into the skillet. While sliding the skillet back and forth rapidly over the heat, quickly stir the eggs with a spatula to spread them continuously over the bottom of the skillet as they thicken.

2 Place the turkey and spinach on top of one half of the eggs, cover the skillet, and cook until the edges thicken and rise, about 1 to 2 minutes.

3 Use a spatula to carefully fold the other half of the eggs over the turkey and spinach. Gently transfer the omelet to a plate, place the avocado slices on top, and serve immediately.

For an anabolic breakfast full of usable protein and nutrients for recovery and muscle growth, try this simple but delicious omelet. With a 1:3 carbs to protein ratio and healthy monounsaturated fats, this is the kind of meal that has you leaving the table feeling powerful!

NUTRITION FACTS

per serving

CALORIES

285

TOTAL FAT

12g

TOTAL CARBS

10g

PROTEIN

32g

PREP TIP *Lightly cook the turkey breast in a frying pan before cooking the eggs to add a smoky flavor.*

I have a boxer friend in Australia who doesn't quite understand what an omelet is, which inspired me to create this dish. It's more of a scramble with a ton of herbs and vegetables held loosely together by eggs. Because she's from down under, of course this "omelet" would be reversed.

NUTRITION FACTS

per serving

CALORIES

350

TOTAL FAT

30g

TOTAL CARBS
10g

PROTEIN
15g

AUSSIE GARDEN & HERB SCRAMBLED OMELET

Makes	2 servings	Serving size	1 omelet	Prep time	5 minutes	Cook time	15 minutes

INGREDIENTS

½ sweet potato

1 tbsp extra virgin olive oil, divided

1 garlic clove, chopped

½ medium yellow onion, diced

⅓ medium zucchini, chopped

⅓ medium yellow squash, chopped

salt and freshly ground black pepper

3 large eggs

1 tbsp chopped fresh parsley

for the mash

½ medium avocado

⅛ cup crumbled feta cheese

DIRECTIONS

1 In a bowl, make the mash by mashing together the avocado and feta with a fork. (Make as smooth or as chunky as you like.) Set aside.

2 Poke holes in the sweet potato, wrap in a paper towel, and heat in the microwave for 3 to 4 minutes. Set aside to cool before cutting into ¼-inch (.5cm) cubes.

3 In a frying pan on the stovetop over medium heat, heat ½ tablespoon of olive oil until shimmering. Add the garlic and onion and sauté until lightly brown, about 3 minutes. Add the zucchini, squash, and cooked sweet potato. Season with salt and pepper. Cook until the vegetables are softened and browned, about 4 to 5 minutes, stirring continuously.

4 In a bowl, beat the eggs vigorously. Add the eggs and the remaining ½ tablespoon of olive oil to the pan. Stir the eggs into the vegetables, cover the pan, and cook until the eggs are set, about 2 to 3 minutes.

5 Remove the omelet from the pan and divide into 2 equal-sized omelets. Sprinkle the parsley over the top and serve immediately with the mash.

PREP TIP // Mix the mash into the egg scramble or smear on toast to eat along with the egg scramble.

SPICY CHORIZO SCRAMBLE

Makes 5 servings | *Serving size* 1 cup | *Prep time* 5 minutes | *Cook time* 20 minutes

Chorizo is an Argentinean asado staple I grew up enjoying at summer cookouts, on sandwiches for lunch, and even in breakfast scrambles. This fatty, salty, and spicy pork sausage dish features eggs, onion, and two kinds of cheeses—with an extra spicy hit from a jalapeño.

INGREDIENTS

¾lb (340g) ground chorizo

½ cup chopped white onion

1 jalapeño, deseeded and flesh chopped

5 large eggs

1 cup shredded Cheddar cheese

½ cup crumbled Cotija cheese

chopped fresh cilantro

DIRECTIONS

1 In a frying pan on the stovetop over medium heat, cook the chorizo until browned and crumbly, about 4 to 5 minutes. Add the onion and jalapeño and cook until the onion is tender, about 8 to 10 minutes.

2 In a bowl, beat the eggs until smooth. Push the chorizo to one side of the pan and pour the eggs into the empty side. Continue cooking until the eggs are scrambled and not runny, about 5 minutes.

3 Fold the chorizo into the cooked eggs, sprinkle the cheeses over the top, and add as much or as little cilantro as desired.

4 Remove the scramble from the pan and serve immediately.

NUTRITION FACTS

per serving

CALORIES

385

TOTAL FAT

30 g

TOTAL CARBS

5 g

PROTEIN

22 g

PREP TIP // *If you buy chorizo in casings, remove the casings and crumble the chorizo.*

I eat this as a typical morning meal on days when I know I'll need to put in some serious effort in the gym or when I need a boost of energy. The slow-release complex carbohydrates are also perfect for long days, hard workouts, or when you wake up with that dragging feeling.

NUTRITION FACTS

per serving

CALORIES
250

TOTAL FAT
10g

TOTAL CARBS
35g

PROTEIN
7g

OMEGA-3 STEEL-CUT OATS

Makes	4 servings	Serving size	½ cup	Prep time	5 minutes	Cook time	20 to 30 minutes

INGREDIENTS

2 cups steel-cut oats

4 cups water

pinch of salt

¼ cup honey (or agave)

1 tbsp flax seeds

1 tsp ground cinnamon

¼ cup crushed walnuts

1 cup blueberries (or strawberries or blackberries)

1 tbsp chia seeds

DIRECTIONS

1 In a saucepan on the stovetop over high heat, bring the oats, water, and salt to a bubbling boil. Reduce the heat to a simmer, cover the pan, and cook until the water is absorbed and the oats are tender, about 20 to 30 minutes. (If the oats appear dry, add extra water as needed.)

2 Transfer the oats to a serving bowl. Stir in the honey, flax seeds, and cinnamon. Top with the walnuts, berries, and chia seeds. Serve immediately. (You can also place the flax seeds on top of the oats and sprinkle the cinnamon over the top.)

PREP TIP *Store covered leftovers in the refrigerator for up to 3 days. Reheat on the stovetop with water or milk until hot.*

I love this for a pre-workout snack (plus a black coffee!) because it's high in carbs and moderate to low in fats and protein—with carbs being the preferred energy macro for high-intensity work. The sweet dried cherries are complemented by the crunchy almonds.

NUTRITION FACTS

per serving

CALORIES

250

TOTAL FAT

9g

TOTAL CARBS

40g

PROTEIN

3g

HOMEMADE CHERRY & ALMOND GRANOLA

Makes 6 squares | **Serving size** 1 square | **Prep time** 5 minutes | **Cook time** 45 minutes

INGREDIENTS

2 cups old-fashioned oats

½ cup dried cherries

½ cup sliced almonds

¼ cup packed dark brown sugar

1 tsp ground cinnamon

½ tsp salt

½ cup agave

2 tbsp melted coconut oil

1 tsp pure vanilla extract

¼ tsp almond extract

DIRECTIONS

1 Preheat the oven to 300°F (149°C).

2 In a bowl, combine all the ingredients and stir until moistened. Spread the mixture onto a baking pan lined with parchment paper and bake until golden, about 45 minutes.

3 Remove the granola from the oven and allow to cool before cutting into six equal-sized squares and serving. (The granola will gain a crunchy texture as it cools.)

PREP TIP Store the granola squares in an airtight container at room temperature for up to 3 weeks.

PUMPKIN & CHIA OVERNIGHT OATS

Makes 1 serving | **Serving size** 1 jar | **Prep time** 8 hours | **Cook time** none

Combining superfoods pumpkin and chia with heart-healthy and energy-providing oats is a win-win, making this a great meal before an early morning workout. Prepare this the night before and enjoy it first thing in the morning on your way out the door to the gym or track or work.

INGREDIENTS

2 tbsp raw organic pumpkin (not filling)

½ cup uncooked old-fashioned oats

½ cup almond milk

2 tsp chia seeds

2 tsp raw organic honey

2 tbsp raw pumpkin seeds

dash of ground cinnamon

dash of ground nutmeg

DIRECTIONS

1 Place the pumpkin in the bottom of a 16-ounce (450-gram) Mason jar. Add the oats, almond milk, chia seeds, and honey, stirring to thoroughly combine. Cover the jar and refrigerate overnight.

2 Remove the jar from the refrigerator and top with the pumpkin seeds, cinnamon, and nutmeg. Serve immediately. (You can eat this hot or cold.)

CHANGE IT UP

Add a scoop of your favorite protein powder for a metabolism boost and drizzle a little honey for sweetness.

NUTRITION FACTS

per serving

CALORIES

375

TOTAL FAT

11g

TOTAL CARBS

58g

PROTEIN

12g

Probiotics in yogurt can improve gut health, which affects your immune system and aids in recovery from hard workouts. This is one of my all-time favorite breakfasts because it provides carbs for training and protein for recovery. It's also low in fat to help with digestion.

NUTRITION FACTS

per serving

CALORIES

450

TOTAL FAT

22g

TOTAL CARBS

40g

PROTEIN

30g

BREAKFASTS

LAYERED YOGURT PARFAIT

| **Makes** 1 serving | **Serving size** 1 parfait | **Prep time** 5 minutes | **Cook time** none |

INGREDIENTS

½ cup fresh or frozen blueberries

1 cup fat-free or 2% plain Greek yogurt, divided

2 tbsp shaved almonds

2 tsp honey

¼ cup toasted granola

dash of ground cinnamon

DIRECTIONS

1 Place the blueberries in the bottom of a parfait glass. Add ½ cup of yogurt over the berries. Layer the almonds on top of the yogurt and drizzle the honey over the top.

2 Add the remaining ½ cup of yogurt over the honey, sprinkle the granola and cinnamon over the top, and serve immediately.

MIKE'S DIRTY WAFFLES

Makes 6 servings | *Serving size* 1 waffle | *Prep time* 5 minutes | *Cook time* 10 minutes

My brother Mike has four boys who are picky eaters and dislike "healthy" foods. These waffles allow him to feed them nutritious ingredients—like eggs and whole-wheat flour—to help them grow and compete. They have usable carbs, fiber, and protein—but go easy on the maple syrup!

INGREDIENTS

2 cups whole-wheat flour

1 tbsp baking powder

½ tsp ground cinnamon

¼ tsp salt

2 large eggs, at room temperature

6 tbsp unsalted butter, melted and slightly cooled

2 tbsp packed light brown sugar

1¾ cups buttermilk

1 tsp pure vanilla extract

DIRECTIONS

1 Preheat the waffle maker to medium-high heat.

2 In a bowl, whisk together the flour, baking powder, cinnamon, and salt.

3 In a separate bowl, whisk together the eggs, butter, brown sugar, buttermilk, and vanilla. Pour the wet ingredients into the dry ingredients and whisk until well combined and no large lumps remain.

4 Pour ⅓ cup of the batter into each well of the waffle maker (or less if your waffle maker is on the smaller side) and close the lid. Cook the waffle until golden and crisp, about 5 to 6 minutes. Repeat this process with the remaining batter to make 6 total waffles.

5 Remove the waffles from the waffle maker, top with your favorite toppings, and serve immediately.

NUTRITION FACTS

per serving

CALORIES

300

TOTAL FAT

15g

TOTAL CARBS

33g

PROTEIN

10g

PREP TIP // *Add 4 tablespoons of flax seeds to the mix to add some healthy omega-3 fatty acids.*

Many restaurants have added this to their menus because it's loaded with healthy monounsaturated fats and heart-healthy fiber. The savory mouthfeel of the avocado is complemented by the acidic spritz of lime juice and the mild heat from the red pepper flakes, creating an explosion of flavors.

AVOCADO TOAST

Makes	1 serving	Serving size	2 slices	Prep time	2 minutes	Cook time	2 to 3 minutes

INGREDIENTS

1 medium ripe avocado

coarse sea salt

cracked black pepper

2 slices whole-grain bread, toasted

juice of 1 small lime

red pepper flakes

DIRECTIONS

1 In a bowl, mash the avocado to your desired consistency and season with salt and pepper. (You can slice the avocado instead.)

2 Spread half the mashed avocado on each slice of toast. Drizzle half the lime juice on each slice and sprinkle as many red pepper flakes as desired over the top. Serve immediately.

NUTRITION FACTS

per serving

CALORIES

350

TOTAL FAT

18g

TOTAL CARBS

41g

PROTEIN

8g

CHANGE IT UP
Top with a poached or fried egg to add some protein and to maximize anabolism.

Almost every New York diner and deli has this breakfast item. This isn't authentic unless the bagel is actually from New York (the best in the world, of course), but you can use bagels from any state or region. While this looks simple, the ingredients create a complex but delicious breakfast.

NEW YORK BAGEL "ALL THE WAY"

Makes	4 servings	Serving size	½ bagel	Prep time	5 minutes	Cook time	none

INGREDIENTS

4oz (110g) cream cheese, softened
2 tbsp capers, drained, plus extra
4oz (110g) sliced smoked salmon
2 plain bagels, split and toasted

1 medium red onion, thinly sliced
freshly ground black pepper
lemon wedges

DIRECTIONS

1 Layer an equal amount of cream cheese, capers, and smoked salmon on each bagel half.

2 Sprinkle a few extra capers over the top of each bagel, add an equal amount of onion to each bagel, and season each bagel with pepper. Serve immediately with lemon wedges.

NUTRITION FACTS

per serving

CALORIES

385

TOTAL FAT
16g

TOTAL CARBS
45g

PROTEIN
16g

CHANGE IT UP
Replace the smoked salmon with lox for a more authentic New York bagel experience.

THE EGG'S NEST

Makes 1 serving | *Serving size* 1 slice | *Prep time* 10 minutes | *Cook time* 5 minutes

INGREDIENTS

unsalted butter

1 slice thick-cut whole-grain bread

1 large egg

salt and freshly ground black pepper

chopped fresh parsley

DIRECTIONS

1 Generously butter a cast iron skillet. Place the skillet on the stovetop over medium-low heat.

2 Use a biscuit cutter to cut a circle from the middle of the bread. Place the bread in the skillet and crack the egg into the circle. Cover the skillet and cook until the egg becomes firm, about 2 minutes. (Cook for 1 minute for a runny egg). Flip and cook to your desired doneness.

3 Remove the egg's nest from the skillet. Season with salt, pepper, and parsley. Serve immediately.

You might know this dish by another name: Egg in a Hole, Egg in a Basket, Bird's Nest, Toad in a Hole, Bull's Eye, One-Eyed Susie, Hole in One—the list goes on. Ultimately, it's a fried egg in the space left by cutting a hole into a piece of bread. This is a great way to cut down on your carb intake.

NUTRITION FACTS

per serving

CALORIES

260

TOTAL FAT

18g

TOTAL CARBS

20g

PROTEIN

10g

Putting pancakes and sweet potatoes together seems like a no-brainer. These hotcakes are hearty and flavorful, and they leave you feeling full and satisfied. Each pancake has complex carbs and fiber, plus tons of beta carotene (a potent antioxidant) found in sweet potato flesh.

NUTRITION FACTS

per serving

CALORIES

260

TOTAL FAT

7 g

TOTAL CARBS

41 g

PROTEIN

9 g

SWEET POTATO HOTCAKES

Makes	6 servings	Serving size	2 pancakes	Prep time	10 minutes	Cook time	90 minutes

INGREDIENTS

1 large sweet potato
2½ cups all-purpose flour
1½ tsp ground cinnamon
1½ tsp ground nutmeg
1 tsp baking powder
1 tsp baking soda
½ tsp salt
2 large eggs

2 cups buttermilk
½ cup whole milk
2 tbsp packed light brown sugar
3 tbsp unsalted butter, melted, plus extra
maple syrup
chopped pecans

DIRECTIONS

1 Preheat the oven to 400°F (204°C).

2 Place the sweet potato on a baking pan and roast until completely soft, about 40 to 50 minutes. Remove the skin, place the potato in a bowl, and mash until creamy. Set aside. (You can roast the sweet potato ahead of time. Refrigerate in a sealed container for up to 3 days.)

3 In a separate bowl, whisk together the flour, cinnamon, nutmeg, baking powder, baking soda, and salt.

4 In a third bowl, whisk together the eggs, buttermilk, milk, and brown sugar. Stir in the sweet potato and butter. Fold the wet ingredients into the dry ingredients and stir until just combined. (The batter will be lumpy—don't overmix.) Let the batter rest for 5 minutes.

5 In a skillet on the stovetop over medium heat, melt a pat of butter to just coat the surface. Add ¼ cup of batter and cook until golden, the edges are set, and bubbles form and burst on the surface, about 2 to 3 minutes. Flip and cook until golden, about 2 minutes more. Repeat this step with the remaining batter to make 12 total pancakes.

6 Remove the pancakes from the skillet, top with maple syrup and pecans (or your favorite toppings), and serve immediately.

PROTEIN PANCAKE

Makes 1 serving | **Serving size** 1 pancake | **Prep time** 10 minutes | **Cook time** 12 minutes

INGREDIENTS

1 cup egg whites
½ cup old-fashioned oats
1 tbsp almond flour
½ tsp ground cinnamon

½ tsp baking powder
1 scoop of protein powder
pinch of salt

DIRECTIONS

1 In a blender on medium speed, blend all the ingredients until well mixed.

2 On a nonstick griddle on the stovetop over medium-high heat, pour the batter in a large circle. Cook until the edges start to look dry, about 2 to 3 minutes. Flip and cook 1 to 2 minutes more.

3 Remove the pancake from the griddle and serve immediately.

When I wake up extra hungry and in need of recovery the day after a hard training session, I turn to this breakfast. This pancake is loaded with protein and carbs to give your body everything it needs to rebuild and grow. This meal is truly an anabolic way to start your day.

NUTRITION FACTS

per serving

CALORIES
315

TOTAL FAT
7 g

TOTAL CARBS
32 g

PROTEIN
33 g

PREP TIP I usually top these with syrup or honey and fruit, but be creative!

CHANGE IT UP
Add 1 tablespoon of flax seeds or flaxseed meal for fiber and omega boosts.

If you need a keto-friendly breakfast, this one has punchy flavors. It's also great if you need a savory dish to meet your caloric needs during hard training. You'll have fun creating this simple dish—and you'll crave more of that crispy bacon, gooey cheese, and warm egg filling.

KNOCKOUT KETO EGG CUPS

Makes	Serving size	Prep time	Cook time
6 servings	2 egg cups	10 minutes	14 minutes

INGREDIENTS

12 slices thick-cut bacon

12 large eggs

salt and freshly ground black pepper

6oz (170g) shredded sharp Cheddar cheese

2 tbsp sliced chives

DIRECTIONS

1 Preheat the oven to 325°F (163°C). Spray a muffin pan with nonstick cooking spray.

2 Cut the bacon slices in half and line each cup of the muffin pan with two pieces. Crack an egg into each cup and season with salt and pepper. Bake until the eggs firm up, about 12 minutes.

3 Remove the egg cups from the oven and preheat the oven to broil. Sprinkle the cheese over the top and broil until the cheese has melted, about 2 minutes.

4 Remove the egg cups from the oven, sprinkle the chives over the top, and serve immediately.

NUTRITION FACTS

per serving

CALORIES

250

TOTAL FAT

18g

TOTAL CARBS

2g

PROTEIN

20g

I'd be remiss to not include a couple keto-friendly recipes for those "fat-heads" (my nickname for ketogenic dieters) out there. These boats are healthy and easy to make. Best of all, they provide the needed fat-laden macronutrient distribution to be a true keto-friendly dish.

NUTRITION FACTS

per serving

CALORIES

300

TOTAL FAT

23g

TOTAL CARBS

7g

PROTEIN

13g

KETO EGG & AVOCADO BOATS

Makes 4 servings | **Serving size** 1 boat | **Prep time** 5 minutes | **Cook time** 18 minutes

INGREDIENTS

2 strips bacon, diced

2 avocados, pitted and halved

4 medium eggs

salt and freshly ground black pepper

grated sharp Cheddar cheese

chopped fresh herbs

DIRECTIONS

1 Preheat the oven to 400°F (204°C).

2 In a skillet on the stovetop over medium heat, cook the bacon until crispy and brown, about 6 minutes, or to your desired doneness.

3 Scoop out 1 to 2 tablespoons of flesh from the avocados to create a larger nest for the eggs. Place the avocados in a baking dish lined with foil or parchment paper, ensuring they fit snugly to prevent them from spilling.

4 Crack an egg into each avocado half. (Reserve some of the egg whites for another use if there's too much egg.) Season with salt and pepper. Top each egg with an equal amount of bacon and cheese.

5 Bake until the whites are set and the yolks are cooked to your liking:
- Softer yolks: 13 to 14 minutes
- Medium yolks: 15 to 16 minutes
- Harder yolks: 17 to 18 minutes

6 Remove the boats from the oven, top with fresh herbs (like chopped parsley or sliced scallions), and serve immediately.

PERFECTLY POACHED EGG

Ever see a perfectly poached egg and wonder how they did that? Now you can find out! Poaching is one of the healthiest and leanest ways to cook an egg because you don't need fats, oils, or high heat. This is a great example of how to add this versatile, delicious, and nutritious food to your diet.

Makes 1 serving | **Serving size** 2 eggs | **Prep time** 10 minutes | **Cook time** 4 minutes

INGREDIENTS

4 tsp white wine vinegar, divided

2 tsp kosher salt, divided

2 large eggs

freshly ground black pepper

DIRECTIONS

1 Fill a small saucepot three-fourths full with water. Place the saucepot on the stovetop over medium heat and bring the water to a simmer. Stir in 2 teaspoons of vinegar and 1 teaspoon of salt.

2 Crack 1 still-cold egg into a bowl. Use a spoon to quickly stir the simmering water in one direction until smoothly spinning around. Carefully slide the egg from the bowl into the center of the whirlpool.

3 Turn off the heat, cover the saucepot, and let sit on the burner for 5 minutes. Carefully remove the egg from the pot with a slotted spoon and place on a paper towel to remove excess water.

4 Repeat these steps with the remaining egg, 2 teaspoons of vinegar, and 1 teaspoon of salt. Serve the eggs immediately.

NUTRITION FACTS
per serving

CALORIES
150

TOTAL FAT
10 g

TOTAL CARBS
1 g

PROTEIN
12 g

PREP TIP // *You can use these poached eggs on Avocado Toast (p. 38) or as a great addition to salads for extra protein.*

This classic dish—which translates to "The Spaniard"—features eggs, onions, potatoes, and fresh herbs. Because it travels well, you can enjoy it hot or cold. Place it between your favorite crispy bread to make a bocadillo for an on-the-go snack or part of a healthy lunch.

NUTRITION FACTS

per serving

CALORIES

375

TOTAL FAT

22g

TOTAL CARBS

35g

PROTEIN

10g

LA ESPAÑOLA

Makes 6 servings | **Serving size** 1 wedge | **Prep time** 10 minutes | **Cook time** 50 minutes

INGREDIENTS

½ cup extra virgin olive oil, plus 2 tbsp

2lb (1kg) white baking potatoes, peeled and cut into ¼-inch (.5cm) slices

salt and freshly ground black pepper

2 medium white Spanish onions, sliced into rings

6 large eggs

2 tbsp chopped fresh parsley

DIRECTIONS

1 In a skillet on the stovetop over medium-low heat, heat ½ cup of olive oil until shimmering. Add half the potato slices and cook until tender, about 15 to 20 minutes, turning occasionally. Transfer the potatoes to a bowl, leaving the oil in the skillet.

2 Cook the remaining potato slices in the oil and transfer to the bowl with the other slices. Leave the oil in the skillet and set aside. Season the potatoes with salt and pepper, gently tossing to coat.

3 In a separate skillet on the stovetop over medium heat, heat the remaining 2 tablespoons of olive oil until shimmering. Add the onion rings and cook until soft and golden, about 15 minutes. Transfer the onions to a plate and allow to cool.

4 In a bowl, whisk the eggs until smooth. Stir in the onions and gently fold in the potatoes.

5 On the stovetop over low heat, heat the reserved oil until shimmering. Add the egg mixture and cook until the sides have started to set and the bottom has turned golden, about 8 to 10 minutes.

6 Loosen the tortilla with a spatula if needed and carefully transfer it to a plate. Turn the skillet upside down and place it onto the uncooked side of the tortilla. Turn the skillet right side up and remove the plate. Return the skillet to the stovetop and continue cooking until the tortilla has set in the center, about 4 minutes.

7 Remove the tortilla from the skillet and allow to cool to room temperature. Cut the tortilla into 6 wedges, sprinkle the parsley over the top, and serve immediately.

THE SPARTAN

Makes 4 servings | *Serving size* 1 wedge | *Prep time* 10 minutes | *Cook time* 20 minutes

I've always loved Mediterranean food, but once I visited Greece, I came home with a new respect and affinity for feta and olive oil. This giant egg dish could feed an army of hungry Spartan warriors. Herbs, cheese, and lots of protein make this a fighter-friendly breakfast or an anabolic snack.

INGREDIENTS

1 tbsp extra virgin olive oil

1 medium zucchini, diced into ½-inch (1.25cm) pieces

2 garlic cloves, finely minced

½ tsp dried basil

¼ tsp dried oregano

coarse ground black pepper

14.5oz (410g) diced tomatoes, drained well

6 large eggs

½ cup grated mozzarella cheese, divided

½ cup crumbled feta cheese, divided

2 tbsp chopped fresh parsley

DIRECTIONS

1 Preheat the oven to broil. Spray an oven-safe heavy frying pan with nonstick cooking spray.

2 Place the pan on the stovetop over medium heat and heat the olive oil until shimmering. Add the zucchini, garlic, basil, and oregano. Season with pepper and sauté for 3 minutes. Add the tomatoes and cook until the liquid is nearly all evaporated, about 3 to 5 minutes more.

3 In a bowl, beat the eggs, pour them over the zucchini, and season with pepper. Cook until the eggs are just starting to set, about 2 to 3 minutes.

4 Add ¼ cup of mozzarella and ¼ cup of feta, stir gently, and cook 3 minutes more. Sprinkle the remaining ¼ cup of mozzarella and ¼ cup of feta over the top. Cover the pan and cook until the feta has mostly melted and the eggs are fairly set, about 3 minutes more.

5 Place the pan in the oven and broil until the top is slightly browned, about 3 minutes.

6 Remove the frittata from the oven and let sit for 3 minutes. Sprinkle the parsley over the top, cut into 4 wedges, and serve immediately.

NUTRITION FACTS

per serving

CALORIES

315

TOTAL FAT

20g

TOTAL CARBS

10g

PROTEIN

25g

With many of my absolute favorite fitness and training ingredients, this hash bursts with colors and nutrients. That makes it an ideal breakfast and a great way to start your day even if you're not a fighter. It's also a versatile dish—add any kind of meat or tofu for a lunch or dinner meal.

NUTRITION FACTS

per serving

CALORIES

200

TOTAL FAT

10g

TOTAL CARBS

20g

PROTEIN

9g

AVOCADO & SWEET POTATO HASH

Makes	4 servings	*Serving size*	¼ of hash and 1 egg	*Prep time*	15 minutes	*Cook time*	25 minutes

INGREDIENTS

1 medium red onion, diced

1 jalapeño, deseeded and flesh sliced

1 tsp red pepper flakes

2 medium sweet potatoes, cut into ¼-inch (.5cm) cubes

salt and freshly ground black pepper

2 cups baby spinach

4 large eggs

1 medium avocado, sliced

1 tbsp chopped fresh parsley

DIRECTIONS

1 Preheat the oven to broil. Spray a cast iron skillet with nonstick cooking spray.

2 Place the skillet on the stovetop over medium heat. Add the onion and jalapeño and sauté until the onion is translucent, about 5 to 7 minutes, stirring frequently. Stir in the red pepper flakes and transfer the mixture to a bowl.

3 Add the sweet potatoes to the still-hot skillet and season with salt and pepper. Cook until soft, about 8 to 10 minutes. Add the spinach and cook until wilted, about 1 to 2 minutes. Add the onion and jalapeño mixture back into the skillet and stir into the potatoes.

4 Crack each of the eggs on one-fourth of the mixture. Place the skillet in the oven and broil until the eggs are set, about 5 to 7 minutes.

5 Remove the hash from the oven, top with the avocado slices, sprinkle the parsley over the top, and serve immediately.

PREP TIP *Use leftover, already-cooked sweet potatoes to make this dish quicker and easier to prepare.*

Yes, you *can* have burritos for breakfast! Colorful and flavorful, this Tex-Mex favorite doesn't hold back on combining traditional burrito ingredients with some enhancements that are sure to help give you a full feeling and an energy boost throughout your morning thanks to the carbs.

SOUTHWEST STEAK & CORN BURRITO

Makes 6 servings | **Serving size** 1 burrito | **Prep time** 10 minutes | **Cook time** 10 minutes

INGREDIENTS

1lb (450g) flank steak

1 cup frozen corn kernels, thawed

½ cup chopped fresh cilantro

2 tbsp minced red onion

2 tbsp freshly squeezed lime juice

1 tbsp extra virgin olive oil

½ tsp cumin

⅛ tsp salt, plus extra

⅛ tsp ground black pepper, plus extra

15oz (420g) black beans, rinsed and drained

6 fat-free flour tortillas

¾ cup shredded Monterey Jack cheese with jalapeño peppers

DIRECTIONS

1 Heat the grill to medium.

2 Place the steak on the grill, season with salt and pepper, and cook to your desired doneness:
- Rare: 2 minutes per side
- Medium rare: 2 to 3 minutes per side
- Medium well: 4 minutes the first side, 2 minutes after turning
- Well done: 5 minutes the first side, 3 minutes after turning

3 In a bowl, combine the corn, cilantro, onion, lime juice, olive oil, cumin, salt, pepper, and beans, stirring well to coat.

4 Remove the steak from the grill, cut into strips, and place an equal amount of steak on each tortilla. Top each tortilla with an equal amount of the corn mixture and cheese.

5 Roll up the tortillas to form burritos and serve immediately.

NUTRITION FACTS

per serving

CALORIES

330

TOTAL FAT

10g

TOTAL CARBS

40g

PROTEIN

21g

EGGS BENEDICT
WITH HOMEMADE HOLLANDAISE

Makes 2 servings | *Serving size* 1 muffin | *Prep time* 15 to 20 minutes | *Cook time* 10 minutes

INGREDIENTS

1 tsp extra virgin olive oil

3 small brown mushrooms, sliced

½ cup chopped spinach

4 tsp white wine vinegar

2 tsp kosher salt

2 large eggs

2 light multigrain English muffins, toasted

1 tbsp grated lemon zest

1 tbsp chopped fresh parsley

for the sauce

4 large eggs, yolks only

1 tbsp freshly squeezed lemon juice

½ cup unsalted butter, melted

pinch of ground cayenne pepper

pinch of kosher salt

DIRECTIONS

1 Fill a small saucepot three-fourths full with water. Place the saucepot on the stovetop over medium heat and bring the water to a simmer. Stir in 2 teaspoons of vinegar and 1 teaspoon of salt.

2 Crack 1 still-cold egg into a bowl. Use a spoon to quickly stir the simmering water in one direction until smoothly spinning around. Carefully slide the egg from the bowl into the center of the whirlpool.

3 Turn off the heat, cover the pot, and let sit on the burner for 5 minutes. Remove the egg with a slotted spoon and place on a paper towel to remove excess water. Repeat steps 2 through 4 with the remaining egg, 2 teaspoons of vinegar, and 1 teaspoon of salt.

4 In a nonstick skillet on the stovetop over medium-high heat, heat the olive oil until shimmering. Add the mushrooms and sauté until tender, about 2 minutes, stirring frequently. Add the spinach and sauté for 2 minutes more. Transfer the vegetables to a bowl.

5 Make the sauce in a steel bowl by whisking together the yolks and lemon juice until the volume doubles. Place the bowl over a small saucepan containing simmering water. Continually whisk as you drizzle in the butter. Remove the bowl from the saucepan and whisk in the cayenne and salt.

6 Add an equal amount of mushrooms, spinach, and egg to each muffin. Top with a dollop of hollandaise and sprinkle an equal amount of lemon zest and parsley over the top. Serve immediately.

This twist on the classic recipe adds sautéed spinach and mushrooms to an English muffin to give you added nutrients and fiber, along with the great flavor you know and love. When adding the hollandaise, keep in mind that it's a high-calorie, high-fat condiment.

NUTRITION FACTS
per serving

CALORIES
350

TOTAL FAT
25 g

TOTAL CARBS
18 g

PROTEIN
17 g

BREAKFASTS

New York City–style delis are such a rarity elsewhere in this country that I feel it's important to include this super-simple staple of NYC cuisine. There's no more perfect breakfast sandwich than the traditional bacon, egg, and cheese that every New Yorker knows all too well.

NUTRITION FACTS

per serving

CALORIES

550

TOTAL FAT

34g

TOTAL CARBS

38g

PROTEIN

30g

THE NEW YORKER

Makes	1 serving	Serving size	1 sandwich	Prep time	5 minutes	Cook time	6 to 8 minutes

INGREDIENTS

2 slices applewood-smoked bacon

½ tbsp unsalted butter

2 large eggs

1 slice American cheese

1 poppy seed Kaiser roll, toasted

DIRECTIONS

1 In a frying pan on the stovetop over medium heat, cook the bacon until crispy and brown, about 2 minutes. Transfer the bacon to a plate lined with paper towels and set aside.

2 In a cast iron skillet on the stovetop over medium heat, melt the butter and crack the eggs into the skillet. Once the whites begin to set after about 1 minute, immediately puncture the yolks.

3 Remove the eggs from the skillet. Top one egg with American cheese and bacon. Place the remaining egg yolk side down on top of the bacon.

4 Transfer the bacon and eggs onto one half of the roll and top with the remaining half. Lightly press together and serve immediately.

CHANGE IT UP
Serve with hot sauce or ketchup or wrap in parchment paper for a portable breakfast.

THE KEVO

Makes 1 serving | **Serving size** 1 omelet | **Prep time** 10 minutes | **Cook time** 5 minutes

INGREDIENTS

½ cup egg whites

pinch of kosher salt

pinch of freshly ground black pepper

1 tsp diced jalapeño

¼ cup organic low-fat cottage cheese, drained

2 tbsp pico de gallo

1 tsp red pepper flakes

DIRECTIONS

1 In a bowl, whisk together the egg whites, salt, and pepper.

2 Spray a skillet with nonstick cooking spray. Place the skillet on the stovetop over medium-high heat and quickly pour the egg mixture into the skillet. While sliding the skillet back and forth rapidly over the heat, quickly stir the eggs with a spatula to spread them over the bottom of the skillet as they thicken. Let sit on the burner for a few seconds to lightly brown the bottom of the omelet. (Don't overcook the eggs; the omelet will continue to cook after folding.)

3 Add the jalapeño and cottage cheese to half the egg, cover the skillet, and cook until the cheese becomes creamy, about 1 to 2 minutes. Fold the other half of the egg over the jalapeño and cottage cheese.

4 Remove the omelet from the skillet, top with the pico de gallo and red pepper flakes, and serve immediately.

Inspired by my boxing advisor and camp coordinator—and son of the legendary Kevin Rooney, who was a welterweight contender and also trained Mike Tyson—this omelet is protein packed, colorful, and spicy! I wasn't sure about the cottage cheese, but once you taste this, you'll be hooked.

NUTRITION FACTS

per serving

CALORIES

200

TOTAL FAT

8 g

TOTAL CARBS

6 g

PROTEIN

26 g

BREAKFASTS

ENTRÉES

Protein benefits your body in many different and vital ways—building and repairing tissues, preparing immune cells, and strengthening bones—but your body can't store this potent macronutrient. It's vital that you consume some protein every day. Almost all the recipes in this chapter have high protein levels—but from sources that will most help your body.

Smells of roasted poultry and fresh herbs in the kitchen always remind me of holiday time in New York. Because Thanksgiving has long been my favorite holiday, this dish lets me have the aromas and flavors of Thanksgiving anytime—but with chicken as a perfect swap.

NUTRITION FACTS

per serving

CALORIES

TOTAL FAT

TOTAL CARBS

PROTEIN

ROASTED CHICKEN
WITH ROSEMARY, GARLIC & ONION

Makes	6 servings	Serving size	6oz (170g)	Prep time	10 minutes	Cook time	2 to 2½ hours

INGREDIENTS

3lb (1.4kg) whole chicken, rinsed and dried

pink Himalayan sea salt and freshly ground black pepper

1 small yellow onion, quartered

1 tbsp chopped fresh rosemary

4 garlic cloves, halved

DIRECTIONS

1 Preheat the oven to 350°F (177°C).

2 Season the chicken with salt and pepper. Stuff the onion and rosemary inside the chicken. Place in a baking pan and add the garlic. Cover with aluminum foil and roast until cooked through and the juices run clear, about 2 to 2½ hours. (The internal temperature should reach at least 165°F [74°C].)

3 Uncover the chicken, increase the oven temperature to broil, and broil for 2 to 4 minutes to crisp the top of the bird.

4 Remove the chicken from the oven, allow to cool slightly, and carve before serving.

SLOW-COOKED SHREDDED CHICKEN

Makes 5 servings | **Serving size** 6oz (170g) | **Prep time** 10 minutes | **Cook time** 6 hours

I love making this meal on "Meal Prep Sundays" because it's versatile—great for lunches, dinners, or low-carb snacks. Add to your favorite rice or grain and pair with some veggies for a well-rounded dinner. Or serve on a toasted roll with melted cheese for a lunch or a snack.

INGREDIENTS

2lb (1kg) chicken breasts

3 garlic cloves, minced

1 medium yellow onion, chopped

1 red or green bell pepper, chopped

1 cup vegetable broth

DIRECTIONS

1 Place the chicken in the bottom of a crockpot. Add the garlic, onion, bell pepper, and broth. Cook until the chicken begins to shred on its own, about 6 hours on low or 3 to 4 hours on high.

2 Remove the chicken from the crockpot and serve immediately. (Shred the chicken with forks as needed.)

NUTRITION FACTS

per serving

CALORIES

275

TOTAL FAT

6g

TOTAL CARBS

2g

PROTEIN

50g

CHANGE IT UP

Use your favorite marinara, barbeque, or teriyaki sauce instead of vegetable broth.

This dish explodes with an incredible amount of fiber and micronutrients. You can make this vegan, vegetarian, or traditional omnivorous based on what you choose to add or take away.
I love this meal because there are endless combinations for making a delicious and nutritious meal.

NUTRITION FACTS

per serving

CALORIES
315

TOTAL FAT
7 g

TOTAL CARBS
32 g

PROTEIN
33 g

BUDDHA BOWL
WITH RED PEPPER DRESSING

Makes	3 servings	Serving size	1 bowl	Prep time	5 minutes	Cook time	10 minutes

INGREDIENTS

1 cup chickpeas

1 tsp extra virgin olive oil

½ tsp smoked paprika

½ tsp turmeric

½ tsp chili powder

½ tsp salt

1 portobello mushroom cap, sliced

8 cherry tomatoes, halved

1½ cups bean sprouts

1 cup cooked quinoa

3 cups mixed greens

1 medium avocado, sliced

½ cup edamame

1 tbsp sesame seeds

for the dressing

12oz (340g) roasted red peppers

1 tbsp extra virgin olive oil

juice of ½ lemon

2 garlic cloves

1 tsp sea salt

1 tsp ground black pepper

DIRECTIONS

1 Preheat the oven to 425°F (218°C).

2 In a bowl, combine the chickpeas, olive oil, paprika, turmeric, chili powder, and salt, gently tossing to evenly coat the chickpeas. Place the mixture on a baking pan lined with parchment paper. Bake until golden, about 20 to 30 minutes. Remove the chickpeas from the oven and set aside to cool.

3 In a blender on high speed, make the dressing by blending the peppers, olive oil, lemon juice, garlic, salt, and pepper until smooth. Taste and adjust the seasonings as needed. Set aside or refrigerate until needed.

4 In a saucepan on the stovetop over medium heat, cook the mushroom and tomatoes until soft and slightly browned, about 3 to 4 minutes. Add the bean sprouts and cook for 1 minute more. Remove the vegetables from the stovetop and allow to cool slightly.

5 Place equal amounts of chickpeas, quinoa, mixed greens, avocado, edamame, mushroom, and tomatoes in 3 bowls. Drizzle the red pepper dressing and sprinkle the sesame seeds over the top. Serve immediately.

When people ask me if I "cheat" during training, I always say: *No, when I want a burger, I have a burger.* But I prepare it myself so I know what goes in it. And this recipe features avocado, which has fats that can help you digest the cholesterol and saturated fats found in the red meat.

NUTRITION FACTS

per serving

CALORIES

580

TOTAL FAT

30g

TOTAL CARBS

33g

PROTEIN

32g

CHAMP CAMP BEEF BURGER

| Makes | 4 servings | Serving size | 4oz (110g) burger | Prep time | 15 minutes | Cook time | 4 to 5 minutes |

INGREDIENTS

1lb (450g) lean ground beef (80%)
1 large egg
½ cup breadcrumbs
½ medium white onion, finely diced
1 tsp Worcestershire sauce
2 tbsp chopped fresh parsley
salt and freshly ground black pepper

4 sesame seed buns
Bibb lettuce
½ medium red onion, sliced
1 medium avocado, quartered and sliced
Dijon mustard
mayonnaise

DIRECTIONS

1 Preheat the grill to high.

2 In a bowl, combine the beef, egg, breadcrumbs, onion, Worcestershire sauce, and parsley. Season with salt and pepper.

3 Form the mixture into 4 patties. Place the patties on the grill and cook until they reach your desired doneness:
• Rare: 2 minutes per side
• Medium rare: 2 to 3 minutes per side
• Medium well: 4 minutes the first side, 2 minutes after turning
• Well done: 5 minutes the first side, 3 minutes after turning

4 Remove the burgers from the grill and place each on a bun half. Top each burger with equal amounts of lettuce, onion, avocado, mustard, and mayonnaise. Top with the remaining bun halves and serve immediately.

GUINNESS-BRAISED SHORT RIB STEW

Makes 8 servings | **Serving size** 6oz (170g) | **Prep time** 15 minutes | **Cook time** 2 hour 30 minutes

Not much is better than perfectly braised, fall-off-the-bone, melt-in-your-mouth short ribs. Add in the sweetness of one of my all-time favorite beers and you get a rich and complex flavor that deserves to be savored. This dish is even better the next day after the flavors sit and mature.

INGREDIENTS

3 tbsp extra virgin olive oil

3lb (1.4kg) boneless beef short ribs, cut into 1½-inch (3.75cm) pieces

kosher salt and freshly ground black pepper

1 large yellow onion, diced

3 garlic cloves, minced

2 carrots, diced

2 celery stalks, cut into ½-inch (1.25cm) pieces

2 cups low-sodium beef stock, divided

1 pint (470ml) Guinness beer

DIRECTIONS

1 In a Dutch oven on the stovetop over medium-high heat, heat the olive oil until shimmering. Season the short ribs with salt and pepper, place in the Dutch oven, and sear until brown, about 5 minutes per side.

2 Remove the ribs from the Dutch oven and set aside. Add the onion and garlic to the Dutch oven and sauté until they're lightly browned, about 5 to 6 minutes, using a wooden spoon to scrape any brown bits from the bottom of the Dutch oven.

3 Add the carrots and celery and cook for 5 minutes more. Add 1 cup of beef stock and continue to scrape the bottom of the Dutch oven.

4 Return the ribs to the Dutch oven and add the beer and the remaining 1 cup of beef stock. Season with salt and pepper, bring to a simmer, and cook uncovered for 20 minutes.

5 Preheat the oven to 380°F (193°C). Cover the Dutch oven, place in the oven, and cook for 2 hours.

6 Remove the stew from the oven and serve immediately.

NUTRITION FACTS

per serving

CALORIES

490

TOTAL FAT

26g

TOTAL CARBS

12g

PROTEIN

46g

Bolognese with rigatoni is one of my favorite Italian dishes and always reminds me of my grandmother and her super-meaty Italian sauce. This twist on the classic uses bison instead of beef. Flavorful ingredients will mask any differences in taste you might experience.

NUTRITION FACTS

per serving

CALORIES
375

TOTAL FAT
10g

TOTAL CARBS
40g

PROTEIN
33g

BISON BOLOGNESE
WITH RIGATONI

Makes	4 servings	Serving size	1 cup pasta and 4oz (110g) bison	Prep time	5 minutes	Cook time	10 minutes

INGREDIENTS

2 tbsp extra virgin olive oil

½ medium yellow onion, diced

1 celery stalk, diced

1 garlic clove, minced

1 tsp red pepper flakes

1lb (450g) lean ground bison (85%)

dash of paprika

salt and freshly ground black pepper

½ cup red wine

30oz (840g) diced tomatoes

2 tbsp chopped fresh oregano, plus 1 tsp

cooked rigatoni

2 tbsp freshly grated Parmesan cheese

2 tbsp chopped fresh parsley

2 tbsp chopped fresh thyme

DIRECTIONS

1 In a saucepan on the stovetop over high heat, heat the olive oil until shimmering. Add the onion, celery, garlic, and red pepper flakes. Sauté until the vegetables begin to soften and brown, about 5 minutes.

2 Add the bison, breaking up the meat into small chunks. Season with paprika, salt, and pepper. Brown until no longer pink, about 2 minutes.

3 Add the red wine, using a wooden spoon to scrape up any brown bits from the bottom, and cook for 3 minutes more.

4 Add the tomatoes and 1 teaspoon of oregano, lower the heat to low, and simmer for 10 minutes more.

5 Remove the Bolognese from the stovetop. Place an equal amount of rigatoni and Bolognese in 4 bowls. Top each bowl with an equal amount of cheese, parsley, thyme, and the remaining 2 tablespoons of oregano. Serve immediately.

CHANGE IT UP
You can serve this bison Bolognese over just about any kind of pasta you like. You can also replace the bison with ground beef.

This healthy twist on a classic will never disappoint—even if it leaves you a sloppy mess. For the same amount of protein, bison is up to 30% leaner than traditional beef. It also has a healthier fatty acid composition because of the diet of the American buffalo. So enjoy this guilt-free dish!

NUTRITION FACTS

per serving

CALORIES

350

TOTAL FAT

17g

TOTAL CARBS

25g

PROTEIN

28g

BISON SLOPPY JOES

Makes	4 servings	Serving size	4oz (110g) meat	Prep time	15 minutes	Cook time	40 minutes

INGREDIENTS

1 tbsp extra virgin olive oil
½ medium white onion, diced
5 garlic cloves, minced
1 red or green bell pepper, diced
1 lb (450g) lean ground bison (85%)
1 cup ketchup

1½ tbsp tomato paste
2 tsp maple syrup
1 tsp Worcestershire sauce
1 tsp liquid smoke
salt and freshly ground black pepper
4 Kaiser rolls

DIRECTIONS

1 In a deep saucepan on the stovetop over medium heat, heat the olive oil until shimmering. Add the onion, garlic, and bell pepper. Cook until the vegetables begin to soften, about 5 to 7 minutes.

2 Add the bison and cook until brown, about 2 minutes, stirring often.

3 Stir in the ketchup, tomato paste, maple syrup, Worcestershire sauce, and liquid smoke. Season with salt and pepper. Let simmer for 25 to 30 minutes. (Add a little water if the meat begins to look dry.)

4 Preheat the oven to broil. Open the rolls, place on a baking pan, and broil for 45 to 70 seconds.

5 Remove the rolls from the oven. Spoon the sloppy joe mixture onto one half of each roll, add any favorite toppings, and top with the other half of each roll. Serve immediately.

CHANGE IT UP
I usually serve this with mixed vegetables to catch the drippings from the sandwich, making for a delicious ending to the meal.

ENTRÉES

66

BROILED LAMB
WITH WHITE BEAN SAUCE

Makes 2 servings | *Serving size* 3 small chops | *Prep time* 2½ hours | *Cook time* 20 minutes

INGREDIENTS

½ cup finely chopped shallots

¼ cup extra virgin olive oil, plus 1 tbsp

3 large garlic cloves, minced

1½ tsp minced fresh rosemary

salt and freshly ground black pepper

6 small lamb loin chops

15oz (420g) cannellini beans, drained

2 plum tomatoes, chopped

½ bunch of fresh spinach, stems removed

DIRECTIONS

1 In a bowl, combine the shallots, ¼ cup of olive oil, garlic, and rosemary. Season with salt and pepper.

2 Arrange the lamb chops in a single layer in a glass baking dish. Spoon the shallot mixture over the chops, turning to coat both sides. Cover and refrigerate for 2 hours.

3 Preheat the oven to broil. Place the lamb chops on a baking pan, reserving the shallot mixture in a saucepan, and broil until medium rare, about 5 minutes per side.

4 In a saucepan on the stovetop over medium heat, bring the reserved shallot mixture to a simmer. Add the beans and tomatoes, stirring to heat through. Season with salt and pepper, cover the pan, and keep warm.

5 In a skillet on the stovetop over high heat, heat the remaining 1 tablespoon of olive oil until shimmering. Add the spinach and sauté until wilted, about 3 minutes. Season with salt and pepper.

6 Remove the lamb chops from the oven. Spoon an equal amount of the bean mixture onto two plates, top with the spinach and lamb chops, and serve immediately.

Lamb was a dish my family would have on Easter, but it eventually became a regular meal because of the ease of cooking. If you want to feel like a gourmet chef without the years of training, lamb is a good place to start. White beans, spinach, and shallots tie all the flavors together beautifully.

NUTRITION FACTS
per serving

CALORIES
690

TOTAL FAT
30g

TOTAL CARBS
15g

PROTEIN
42g

ENTRÉES

This spicy and savory dish is a fan favorite in my household, where a little heat is always welcome. The capsaicin that gives cayenne its spice has a tremendous thermic effect in the body and can help boost your metabolism and thus your body's natural fat-burning capabilities.

CURRY & CAYENNE COCONUT SHRIMP

Makes	4 servings	Serving size	4oz (110g)	Prep time	10 minutes	Cook time	5 minutes

INGREDIENTS

1lb (450g) shrimp, peeled and deveined

1 tbsp curry powder

1 tsp ground cayenne pepper

1 tsp paprika

salt and freshly ground black pepper

2 tbsp coconut oil

DIRECTIONS

1 In a bowl, combine the shrimp, curry powder, cayenne, and paprika. Season with salt and pepper, tossing to coat.

2 In a cast iron skillet on the stovetop over medium-high heat, heat the coconut oil until shimmering. Add the shrimp and cook until firm, about 2½ minutes per side.

3 Remove the shrimp from the skillet and serve immediately.

NUTRITION FACTS

per serving

CALORIES

130

TOTAL FAT

7 g

TOTAL CARBS

0 g

PROTEIN

 g

CHANGE IT UP
Pair this with stir-fry vegetables and jasmine rice for an Asian-inspired meal.

Every time I'd see this on a menu while dining out, I'd have to order it. I decided I needed to figure out how to prepare it myself. This crispy yet juicy cod dish has a tremendous amount of flavor and a mouthfeel that's sure to impress any dinner guests you might be hosting.

MISO-GLAZED COD

Makes	2 servings	Serving size	1 fillet	Prep time	10 minutes	Cook time	15 minutes

INGREDIENTS

3 tbsp white miso paste

2 tbsp mirin

2 tbsp sake

1 tbsp water

1 tsp packed light brown sugar

unsalted butter

2 cod fillets, about 7oz (200g) each

DIRECTIONS

1 In a skillet on the stovetop over medium heat, whisk together the miso paste, mirin, sake, water, and brown sugar until the mixture simmers and thickens slightly, about 1 to 3 minutes. Remove the miso mixture from the stovetop and allow to cool completely.

2 Place the fillets on the baking pan and brush with the miso mixture. Rest the fillets at room temperature to marinate, about 15 to 20 minutes.

3 Move an oven rack to about 6 inches (15.25cm) from the heat source and preheat the oven to broil. Line a baking pan with aluminum foil and lightly grease the aluminum foil with butter.

4 Place the pan in the oven and broil for 5 minutes. Turn the pan 180° and broil until the fish flakes easily with a fork, about 5 minutes more.

5 Remove the fish from the oven, remove the pin bones from the fish, and serve immediately.

NUTRITION FACTS

per serving

CALORIES

260

TOTAL FAT

4 g

TOTAL CARBS

15 g

PROTEIN

33 g

OVEN-ROASTED FLOUNDER

Makes 2 servings | **Serving size** 5oz (140g) fillet | **Prep time** 10 minutes | **Cook time** 20 minutes

Flounder is one of my favorite white fish because of its ease of cooking and its ability to take on the flavor of whatever it's prepared with—in this case, Parmesan and thyme. This recipe also uses breadcrumbs to create a crispy crunch that's sure to leave you satisfied.

INGREDIENTS

2 flounder fillets, about 5oz (140g) each

1/4 cup unsalted butter, melted, divided

1 cup panko breadcrumbs

2/3 cup grated Parmesan cheese

1/2 tsp salt

1/2 tsp ground black pepper

1/2 tsp dried thyme

DIRECTIONS

1 Preheat the oven to 400°F (204°C). Spray a shallow baking dish with nonstick cooking spray.

2 Arrange the fillets in the dish and brush with 1/2 tablespoon of butter.

3 In a bowl, combine the breadcrumbs, cheese, salt, pepper, thyme, and the remaining 3 1/2 tablespoons of butter. Sprinkle the mixture over the fish and bake until it flakes easily with a fork, about 15 to 20 minutes.

4 Remove the fish from the oven and serve immediately.

NUTRITION FACTS
per serving

CALORIES

330

TOTAL FAT

17g

TOTAL CARBS

20g

PROTEIN

30g

CHANGE IT UP
Pair this fish dish with Spicy Zoodles (p. 101) and Garlic & Rosemary Roasted Potatoes (p. 94).

ENTRÉES

Because my mother was born in Argentina and because I come from a long line of asado-loving gauchos, this dish is near and dear to my family and culture. Chimichurri is a staple sauce of many Argentine dishes and is an oil-based, garlic-centric garnish for the flank steak.

ARGENTINEAN-STYLE FLANK STEAK
WITH CHIMICHURRI

Makes 4 steaks | *Serving size* 1 steak | *Prep time* 15 minutes | *Cook time* 8 minutes

INGREDIENTS

4 flank steaks, about 6oz (170g) each

kosher salt and freshly ground black pepper

2 tbsp unsalted butter

for the sauce

1 cup chopped fresh parsley

5 garlic cloves, minced

½ cup extra virgin olive oil

¼ cup red wine vinegar

¼ tsp red pepper flakes

1 tsp fine sea salt

2 tbsp water

DIRECTIONS

1 Preheat the grill to medium. Season both sides of the steaks with salt and pepper.

2 Place the steaks directly on the grill, top each with ½ tablespoon of butter, and cook until well seared and dark brown, about 5 to 7 minutes. Flip and continue grilling until the steaks reach your desired doneness:
- Rare: 2 to 3 minutes
- Medium rare: 3 to 4 minutes
- Medium well: 5 to 6 minutes
- Well done: 7 to 8 minutes

3 Make the sauce in a food processor fitted with a steel blade by blending the parsley and garlic until finely chopped, stopping as necessary to scrape the sides of the bowl. Transfer the mixture to a bowl. Whisk in the olive oil, vinegar, red pepper flakes, sea salt, and water. (You can strengthen the taste by refrigerating this overnight.)

4 Remove the steaks from the grill, slice as desired, and serve immediately with the chimichurri. (You can also serve the sauce on toasted Italian bread.)

PREP TIP *Grilling with large-grain salt gives the outside of the meat that crunchy char that the best steakhouses have.*

This dish features mushrooms and an onion cooked in butter and Worcestershire sauce drizzled over skirt steak. The sauce—combined with a succulent and well-marbled steak—makes this rich and savory meal great for cold nights when your body needs that warm and full feeling.

MUSHROOM & ONION–SLATHERED SKIRT STEAK

Makes 4 servings | **Serving size** 1 steak | **Prep time** 20 minutes | **Cook time** 25 minutes

NUTRITION FACTS

per serving

CALORIES

375

TOTAL FAT

25g

TOTAL CARBS

3g

PROTEIN

28g

INGREDIENTS

4 skirt steaks, about 4oz (110g) each

kosher salt and freshly ground black pepper

2 tbsp unsalted butter, divided

8oz (225g) sliced mushrooms

1 medium yellow onion, halved and sliced

3 tbsp Worcestershire sauce

DIRECTIONS

1 Preheat the oven to broil. Season the steak with salt and pepper.

2 In a deep-dish pan, place the steaks. Top each with ¼ tablespoon of butter. Broil until the steaks reach your desired doneness:
- Rare: 3 minutes per side
- Medium rare: 4 minutes first side, 3 minutes after turning
- Medium well: 5 minutes first side, 3 minutes after turning
- Well done: 5 minutes first side, 5 minutes after turning

3 In a saucepan on the stovetop over medium heat, sauté the mushrooms, onion, and the remaining 1 tablespoon of butter until the onion becomes soft and translucent, about 5 to 7 minutes. Add the Worcestershire sauce, tossing to combine.

4 Remove the steak from the oven and slather each steak with an equal amount of mushrooms and onion. Serve immediately.

CHANGE IT UP
This goes great with Grilled Balsamic Asparagus (p. 97) or Charred Broccoli (p. 106).

PERFECTLY BROILED SALMON

Makes 4 servings | *Serving size* 1 fillet | *Prep time* 5 minutes | *Cook time* 10 minutes

INGREDIENTS

4 wild-caught, center-cut salmon fillets, about 6oz (170g) each

1 tbsp extra virgin olive oil

1 lemon, sliced

salt and freshly ground black pepper

chopped fresh parsley

DIRECTIONS

1 Preheat the oven to broil. Pat the salmon dry with paper towels. (Drier salmon makes for crispier fish.) Cover a baking pan with aluminum foil and spray with nonstick cooking spray.

2 Place the fillets skin side down on the pan. Brush with the olive oil, top with lemon slices, and season with salt and pepper. Fold the foil over the fish to trap in the heat and to protect the skin from cooking too quickly.

3 Broil the fish until it reaches your desired doneness:
- Rare: 7 to 8 minutes
- Medium well: 8 to 10 minutes
- Well done: 10 to 12 minutes

4 Unwrap the foil and broil for 2 minutes more to crisp the top.

5 Remove the fish from the oven, top with parsley, and serve immediately.

I was often afraid to cook salmon because it didn't seem as good as what a restaurant made. Once I figured out this recipe, I never ordered salmon again. The key is to crisp the outside but allow the flesh to stay moist and flavorful. Salmon needs little seasoning, but it must cook properly.

NUTRITION FACTS

per serving

CALORIES
285

TOTAL FAT
18g

TOTAL CARBS
0g

PROTEIN
30g

Featuring the nuttiness of fresh figs, this herbaceous pizza also offers the pungent and sometimes bitter flavor of arugula paired with the sweetness of a balsamic glaze. Figs are rich in B vitamins, magnesium, phosphorous, and iron. They're also high in antioxidants and fiber.

NUTRITION FACTS

per serving

CALORIES

350

TOTAL FAT

18g

TOTAL CARBS

40g

PROTEIN

8g

ENTRÉES

BALSAMIC-GLAZED FIG & ARUGULA PIZZA

| Makes | 8 slices | Serving size | 2 slices | Prep time | 20 minutes | Cook time | 40 minutes |

INGREDIENTS

1 head of garlic

2 tbsp extra virgin olive oil, plus ½ tsp

1 medium red onion, thinly sliced

pinch of salt

1 cup crumbled Gorgonzola cheese

16oz (450g) pizza dough

6 figs, quartered

¼ cup Kalamata olives

dried oregano

2 cups finely chopped arugula

for the glaze

1 cup balsamic vinegar

¼ cup packed light brown sugar

DIRECTIONS

1 Preheat the oven to 400°F (204°C). Cut the top off the head of garlic, place in aluminum foil, and drizzle ½ teaspoon of olive oil over the top. Wrap up the foil and roast until the garlic is slightly browned and creamy, about 15 minutes. Remove the garlic from the oven and set aside.

2 In a saucepan on the stovetop over medium heat, make the glaze by combining the vinegar and brown sugar. Stir constantly until the sugar has dissolved. Bring to a boil, reduce the heat to low, and simmer until the glaze is reduced by half, about 20 minutes. (The glaze should coat the back of a spoon.) Remove the glaze from the stovetop and let cool. Pour into a 16-ounce (450g) Mason jar, cover the jar, and refrigerate.

3 In a skillet on the stovetop over medium-high heat, heat the remaining 2 tablespoons of olive oil until shimmering. Add the onion and sauté for 3 minutes, stirring frequently. Lower the heat to medium and add the salt. Sauté until the onion begins to caramelized and soften, about 10 minutes.

4 Preheat the oven to 450°F (232°C). Roll out the dough into a circle and place on a pizza stone. Rub with the garlic and sprinkle the cheese over the top. Top with the figs, onion, and olives and season with oregano. Bake until the cheese begins to brown, about 9 to 11 minutes.

5 Remove the pizza from the oven. Sprinkle the arugula over the top and drizzle the chilled glaze over the top. Cut the pizza into 8 equal-sized slices and serve immediately.

As a big fan of Greek culture and cuisine and also being from New York, I had to figure out how to make the prototypical New York gyro. The real trick here is the tzatziki sauce that bursts with cucumber and Greek yogurt and complements the flavors of the marinade.

NUTRITION FACTS

per serving

CALORIES

450

TOTAL FAT

12g

TOTAL CARBS

44g

PROTEIN

42g

GRILLED CHICKEN GYRO
WITH TZATZIKI SAUCE

Makes 4 servings	**Serving size** 1 pita	**Prep time** 24 hours	**Cook time** 15 minutes

INGREDIENTS

2lb (1kg) chicken breasts, cut into pieces

4 pita pockets

4 romaine leaves, chopped

for the marinade

¼ cup plain Greek yogurt

3 tbsp freshly squeezed lemon juice

2 tbsp extra virgin olive oil

1 tbsp red wine vinegar

1½ tsp salt

1 tsp ground black pepper

2 tsp dried oregano

for the sauce

1½ cups plain Greek yogurt

2 tbsp extra virgin olive oil

1 tbsp freshly squeezed lemon juice

1 tbsp red wine vinegar

2 tsp salt, plus extra

1 tbsp chopped fresh dill

3 garlic cloves, finely diced

1 cucumber, grated and squeezed to drain

freshly ground black pepper

DIRECTIONS

1 In a bowl, make the marinade by combining all the marinade ingredients. Pour the marinade into a resealable plastic bag and add the chicken. Refrigerate for at least 30 minutes but preferably for 24 hours.

2 In a separate bowl, make the tzatziki sauce by combining the Greek yogurt, olive oil, lemon juice, vinegar, salt, dill, and garlic. Stir in the cucumber and season with salt and pepper. Set aside.

3 Heat the grill to medium. Thread the chicken onto kebab skewers and grill until fully cooked, about 5 to 7 minutes per side.

4 Remove the chicken from the grill and from the skewers and place equal amounts in each pita pocket. Top each with an equal amounts of tzatziki sauce and romaine. Serve immediately.

PREP TIP *Warm the pita pockets in a frying pan on the stovetop or in the microwave for 20 to 30 seconds to make them more pliable.*

MEDITERRANEAN-STYLE GRILLED CHICKEN
WITH PENNE

Makes 6 servings | **Serving size** 5oz (140g) | **Prep time** 5 minutes | **Cook time** 15 minutes

Whether you're looking for a whole meal with protein and carbs or just a protein entrée, this recipe is a great addition to your culinary arsenal. Just 1 cup of cooked penne boosts the carbs by more than 40 compared with the chicken alone. Plus, the chicken offers plenty of protein.

INGREDIENTS

2 tbsp extra virgin olive oil

½ cup white wine, plus 2 tbsp

6 skinless, boneless chicken breasts

3 garlic cloves, minced

½ cup diced white onion

3 cups tomatoes, chopped

2 tsp chopped fresh thyme

1 tbsp chopped fresh basil

¼ tbsp chopped fresh parsley

3 tbsp chopped black olives

salt and freshly ground black pepper

cooked penne

DIRECTIONS

1 In a skillet on the stovetop over medium heat, heat the olive oil and 2 tablespoons of white wine until shimmering. Add the chicken and sauté until golden, about 4 to 6 minutes per side. Remove the chicken from the skillet and set aside.

2 Add the garlic to the still-hot skillet and sauté for 30 seconds. Add the onion and sauté for 3 minutes more. Add the tomatoes and bring everything to a boil. Lower the heat to low, add the remaining ½ cup of white wine, and simmer for 10 minutes. Add the thyme and basil and simmer for 5 minutes more.

3 Return the chicken to the skillet and cover. Cook over low heat until the chicken is cooked through and no longer pink inside, about 1 to 2 minutes. Add the parsley and olives, season with salt and pepper, and cook for 1 minute more.

4 Remove the chicken, vegetables, and herbs from the skillet, spoon them over the penne, and serve immediately.

CHANGE IT UP
Use whole-wheat pasta or spaghetti squash to cut impact carbs.

NUTRITION FACTS
per serving

CALORIES

420

TOTAL FAT

9g

TOTAL CARBS

50g

PROTEIN

37g

Red snapper is quite the intimidating-looking fish before cooking, but once it's been prepared properly, it creates a beautiful dish with an abundance of flavor. This highly versatile and firm-fleshed fish is the perfect entrée protein for seafood lovers the world over.

NUTRITION FACTS

per serving

CALORIES

270

TOTAL FAT

16g

TOTAL CARBS

0g

PROTEIN

30g

CRISPY RED SNAPPER

Makes	3 servings	Serving size	5oz (140g) fillet	Prep time	60 minutes	Cook time	6 minutes

INGREDIENTS

1lb (450g) fresh red snapper fillets

large pinch of salt, plus extra

2 tbsp vegetable oil, divided

freshly ground black pepper

juice of 1 lemon, divided

chopped fresh parsley

DIRECTIONS

1 Place the fillets skin side up on a plate and refrigerate uncovered for 1 hour. (This dries out the skin and is a crucial step.)

2 In a stainless steel skillet on the stovetop over high heat, heat the salt and 1 tablespoon of vegetable oil until the oil begins to smoke. Remove the skillet from the stovetop and wipe with a clean kitchen towel. (This creates a temporary seal on the skillet—a makeshift nonstick surface.)

3 Season both sides of the fillets with salt. Return the skillet to the stovetop and heat the remaining 1 tablespoon of vegetable oil. Once the oil is smoking, add 1 fillet, lowering it into the skillet skin side down and away from you. Press gently with a spatula until the fillet no longer wants to curl up and the entire skin side is flush with the skillet, ensuring complete and direct contact.

4 Cook the fillet until nearly cooked through, about 3 minutes, pressing periodically with a spatula. (The fish should still be opaque and a bit raw at the thickest part.) Gently turn the fish (working away from you so the oil doesn't splash on you), remove the skillet from the stovetop, and allow to cook off the heat for about 1 minute more. Repeat this cooking process with the remaining fillets.

5 Remove the fillets from the skillet and season with salt and pepper. Splash an equal amount of lemon juice on each fillet, sprinkle an equal amount of parsley on top of each fillet, and serve immediately.

This is a super-fast and easy meal that comes out restaurant-quality each and every time! Tuna has a tremendous protein content and also contains heart-healthy omega-3 fatty acids, which can greatly aid recovery after hard workouts or quell those hunger pangs after a long day.

NUTRITION FACTS

per serving

CALORIES

350

TOTAL FAT

21g

TOTAL CARBS

5g

PROTEIN

31g

SESAME-CRUSTED TUNA STEAK

Makes	4 servings	Serving size	6oz (170g) steak	Prep time	5 minutes	Cook time	10 minutes

INGREDIENTS

2 tsp sesame oil

2 tbsp liquid aminos

4 sushi-grade tuna steaks, about 6oz (170g) each and 1-inch (2.5cm) thick

salt and freshly ground black pepper

⅓ cup white sesame seeds

¼ cup black sesame seeds

2 tbsp vegetable oil

2 cups fresh field greens

DIRECTIONS

1 In a bowl, whisk together the sesame oil and aminos. Season each tuna steak with salt and pepper. Using a spoon, drizzle a little of the mixture over each steak and rub with the back of a spoon to cover the entire surface. Flip each steak and repeat this process.

2 On a plate, combine the white and black sesame seeds and spread them into a thin layer. Place the steaks on the sesame seeds, press down to cover the fish evenly and completely, and flip to cover the other side.

3 In a heavy frying pan on the stovetop over medium-high heat, heat the vegetable oil until shimmering. Add 2 steaks and sear until the white sesame seeds start to turn golden, about 1 to 1½ minutes per side. (If desired, you can use tongs to gently support the steaks and sear the edges or leave them visibly rare [which is my preference].) Repeat this cooking process with the remaining steaks.

4 Remove the steaks from the pan and cut into thin slices. Place an equal amount of fresh greens on 4 plates and top each with an equal of tuna. Serve immediately.

PREP TIP *You can top the steaks with soy sauce, wasabi, or your favorite ginger or teriyaki dressing.*

PANKO-CRUSTED BAKED COD

Makes **3** servings | Serving size **1** fillet | Prep time **10** minutes | Cook time **12** minutes

INGREDIENTS

1 large egg

⅓ cup panko breadcrumbs

1 tsp finely chopped fresh parsley

1 tsp minced garlic

salt and freshly ground black pepper

3 cod fillets, about 6oz (170g) each

1 lemon, sliced

DIRECTIONS

1 Preheat the oven to 425°F (218°C). Spray a baking pan with nonstick cooking spray.

2 In a bowl, whisk the egg and pour into a deep dish.

3 In a separate deep dish, mix the breadcrumbs, parsley, and garlic. Season with salt and pepper. Dip the cod fillets in the egg until coated and lightly bread with the panko.

4 Place the fish on the pan and top each with a lemon slice. Bake until browned and the fish is cooked through, about 12 minutes.

5 Remove the cod from the oven and serve immediately.

CHANGE IT UP
This is also great for fish tacos. Cut into thinner pieces and top with red cabbage, pico de gallo, and avocado.

This lightly breaded and minimally fried cod with fresh lemon and parsley is a great dish for making a fish lover out of anyone. The crispy, lemony flavor combined with the soft, flaky, and almost buttery flesh of the cod makes this a meal you'll want to put on weekly rotation.

NUTRITION FACTS

per serving

CALORIES
200

TOTAL FAT
8g

TOTAL CARBS
5g

PROTEIN
30g

ENTRÉES

Fighters I work with love these meatballs because they make you feel like you're "cheating" when you're not. Turkey is lower in fat (especially saturated fat) than other poultry—but not in flavor. I hope you enjoy this healthy and fit twist on my Italian grandmother's meatball recipe.

NUTRITION FACTS

per serving

CALORIES

21

TOTAL FAT

12 g

TOTAL CARBS

2 g

PROTEIN

23 g

ITALIAN TURKEY MEATBALLS

Makes	5 servings	Serving size	4 meatballs	Prep time	10 minutes	Cook time	30 minutes

INGREDIENTS

2lb (1kg) lean ground turkey (99%)

1 tsp minced garlic

2 large eggs

1 cup breadcrumbs

1 tbsp Italian seasoning

¼ cup grated Parmesan cheese

⅓ cup chopped fresh parsley

2 tbsp chopped fresh basil

salt and freshly ground black pepper

DIRECTIONS

1 Preheat the oven to 350°F (177°C).

2 In a bowl, combine the turkey, garlic, eggs, breadcrumbs, Italian seasoning, cheese, parsley, and basil. Season with salt and pepper.

3 Form the mixture into 20 equal-sized meatballs and place on a baking pan lined with parchment paper. Bake until no longer pink inside, about 28 to 30 minutes, checking occasionally with a toothpick.

4 Remove the meatballs from the oven and serve immediately.

CHANGE IT UP
Serve these with pasta and sauce, in hoagies, or with Spicy Zoodles (p. 101).

There's nothing like a fresh batch of hot chili on a cold Sunday while watching football! It's also great when having company or for taking to a friend's house. I'll even use leftovers as a side dish for meals. This lean, protein-rich meal packs a punch of spice that's sure to clear out your nostrils!

NUTRITION FACTS

per serving

CALORIES

250

TOTAL FAT

10g

TOTAL CARBS

19g

PROTEIN

22g

SPICY TURKEY CHILI

Makes	4 servings	Serving size	¾ cup	Prep time	15 minutes	Cook time	45 minutes

INGREDIENTS

1½ tbsp extra virgin olive oil

1lb (450g) lean ground turkey (99%)

1 medium white onion, chopped

2 cups water

28oz (800g) crushed tomatoes

15oz (420g) kidney beans

1 tbsp minced garlic

½ tsp paprika

½ tsp chili powder

½ tsp ground cayenne pepper

½ tsp cumin

½ tsp salt

½ tsp ground black pepper

½ tsp dried oregano

shredded sharp Cheddar cheese

DIRECTIONS

1 In a pot on the stovetop over medium heat, heat the olive oil until shimmering. Add the turkey and cook until browned, about 2 minutes. Stir in the onion and cook until tender, about 5 to 7 minutes.

2 Add the water, tomatoes, kidney beans, garlic, paprika, chili powder, cayenne, cumin, salt, pepper, and oregano. Bring to a boil, reduce the heat to low, cover the pot, and simmer for 30 minutes.

3 Remove the chili from the stovetop. Spoon equal amounts into 4 serving bowls, top with cheese, and serve immediately.

BBQ GROUND TURKEY

Makes	5 servings	Serving size	5oz (140g) meat and 2 lettuce leaves	Prep time	15 minutes	Cook time	10 minutes

I created this recipe by accident when I ran out of marinara sauce to make my turkey version of sloppy joes. Now I have a barbecue turkey dish that my nephews love. Because this sauce is considerably sweeter than marinara, you can eat the meat on a crispy romaine leaf.

INGREDIENTS

1lb (450g) lean ground turkey (99%)

1 green bell pepper, chopped

1 medium red onion, chopped

1 tomato, diced

1 cup barbecue sauce

1 tsp red pepper flakes

freshly ground black pepper

1 romaine heart

DIRECTIONS

1 In a nonstick skillet on the stovetop over medium heat, cook the turkey, pepper, onion, and tomato until the turkey is crumbly and no longer pink, about 5 minutes.

2 Stir in the barbecue sauce and red pepper flakes. Season with pepper. Reduce the heat to low and simmer for 10 minutes, stirring occasionally.

3 Remove the turkey from the stovetop. Place 2 romaine leaves each on 5 plates, add an equal amount of turkey to each, and serve immediately.

CHANGE IT UP
You can serve with vegetables and rice; on a roll or a hoagie; in a wrap or a pita; or in soft or hard tacos.

NUTRITION FACTS
per serving

CALORIES

250

TOTAL FAT

8 g

TOTAL CARBS

10 g

PROTEIN

35 g

Packed with tons of colorful veggies and protein-laden tofu, this is a must-have recipe for vegetarian and vegan athletes. I imposed a weekly vegetarian dinner for my family years ago to help keep us healthy and fit. It has since become one of the favorite nights of the week.

NUTRITION FACTS

per serving

CALORIES

150

TOTAL FAT

13g

TOTAL CARBS

6g

PROTEIN

6g

TERIYAKI TOFU STIR-FRY

Makes **4** servings | Serving **size** 1 to 1½ cups | **Prep time** 20 minutes | **Cook time** 20 minutes

INGREDIENTS

1½ tbsp sesame oil, divided

1 block firm extra-protein tofu, patted dry with paper towels and cubed

3 cups broccoli florets

2 large zucchinis, quartered and cut into ½-inch (1.25cm) slices

¼ scallion, diced

2 carrots, sliced

½ red bell pepper, sliced

5 to 6 bok choy stalks, ribs removed and leaves sliced into 1-inch (2.5cm) strips

2 cups bean sprouts

for the sauce

1¼ cups cold water, divided

¼ cup soy sauce

5 tsp packed light brown sugar

1 tbsp honey

½ tsp ground ginger

1 garlic clove, minced

2 tbsp cornstarch

DIRECTIONS

1 In a saucepan on the stovetop over medium heat, make the sauce by combining 1 cup of water, soy sauce, brown sugar, honey, ginger, and garlic. Cook until nearly heated through, about 1 minute.

2 In a bowl, combine the cornstarch and the remaining ¼ cup of water and stir until dissolved. Add the cornstarch mixture to the saucepan and cook until thickened, about 5 to 7 minutes, stirring often.

3 In a separate saucepan on the stovetop over medium heat, heat ½ tablespoon of sesame oil until shimmering. Add the tofu and cook until golden, about 10 minutes. (Cover and reduce the heat to low to dry out the tofu more.) Remove the tofu from the saucepan, transfer to a bowl, and drizzle half the teriyaki sauce over the tofu, tossing until coated. Set aside the tofu and the remaining sauce.

4 In a wok on the stovetop over medium-high heat, heat the remaining 1 tablespoon of sesame oil until shimmering. Add the broccoli, zucchinis, scallion, carrots, and bell pepper and cook until tender, about 8 to 10 minutes. Add the bok choy and bean sprouts and cook until slightly wilted, about 2 minutes more.

5 Add the tofu, drizzle the remaining sauce over the top, and toss to combine. Remove the stir-fry from the stovetop. Serve immediately with your favorite rice or noodle.

When I'm getting close to a fight, carb intake becomes specifically timed. To make training camp more enjoyable, I begin incorporating a lot of low-carb versions of my favorite dishes. This is great on its own or in combination with other dishes, including meatballs.

NUTRITION FACTS

per serving

CALORIES

TOTAL FAT

g

TOTAL CARBS

16g

PROTEIN

1g

LOW-CARB SPAGHETTI SQUASH

| **Makes** 3 servings | **Serving size** 1½ cups cooked | **Prep time** 10 minutes | **Cook time** 50 minutes |

INGREDIENTS

1 medium spaghetti squash

1 tbsp extra virgin olive oil

salt and freshly ground black pepper

fresh herbs, optional

DIRECTIONS

1 Preheat the oven to 375°F (191°C).

2 Using a heavy chef's knife, cut the squash in half lengthwise and use a spoon to scoop out the seeds. Lightly drizzle the cut side of each squash with olive oil and season with salt and pepper.

3 Place the squash halves cut side down on a baking pan lined with parchment paper. Bake until soft and easily pierced with a knife, about 40 to 50 minutes.

4 Remove the squash from the oven, flip to face them cut side up, and allow to cool for 5 minutes.

5 Run a fork through the flesh to create spaghetti-shaped noodles and serve immediately.

PREP TIP *Toss with your favorite marinara sauce or use butter, garlic, and your favorite herbs to make this feel more like pasta.*

MORNING GLORY PIZZA

| **Makes** 4 small pizzas | **Serving size** 1 pizza | **Prep time** 35 minutes | **Cook time** 12 minutes |

I'm not really a pizza guy (weird being that my father is Italian and I'm from New York), but I've taken healthier pizza ingredients and combined them with my favorite breakfast foods: bacon, eggs, tomatoes, spinach, and cheese. And now you have a pizza perfect for mornings or for anytime.

INGREDIENTS

2 strips center-cut bacon

1 cup all-purpose or white whole-wheat flour, plus extra

1½ tsp baking powder

½ tsp kosher salt, plus extra

1 cup nonfat Greek yogurt, drained

baby spinach

½ cup shredded mozzarella cheese

8 cherry tomatoes, sliced

4 large eggs

freshly ground black pepper

DIRECTIONS

1 Preheat the oven to 450°F (232°C). Line a baking pan with parchment paper and spray with nonstick cooking spray.

2 In a frying pan on the stovetop over medium heat, cook the bacon until crispy and brown, about 2 minutes per side. Remove the bacon from the stovetop and place on paper towels until needed.

3 In a bowl, whisk together the flour, baking powder, and salt. Add the yogurt and mix with a fork until the mixture looks like small crumbles.

4 Lightly dust a work surface with flour and placed the dough on the flour. Knead the dough a few times until tacky but not sticky, about 20 turns, turning the dough 90° after pressing down each time. (You shouldn't have dough on your hands when you pull them away from the dough.)

5 Divide the dough into 4 equal-sized balls. Sprinkle the work surface with extra flour and use a rolling pin with a little flour on it to roll the dough into thin rounds that are 7 to 8 inches (17.5cm to 20cm) in diameter.

6 Place the rounds on the baking pan and top each with equal amounts of spinach, cheese, and tomatoes, leaving the center open for an egg. Gently break an egg into the center of each round and top each with an equal amount of bacon. Season with salt and pepper.

7 Bake until the crusts are golden and the eggs have set, about 10 to 12 minutes.

8 Remove the pizzas from the oven and serve immediately.

NUTRITION FACTS

per serving

CALORIES

270

TOTAL FAT

9 g

TOTAL CARBS

27 g

PROTEIN

20 g

ENTRÉES

SALADS & SIDES

These aren't your typical salads and side dishes. They turn many typical salad and side ingredients into new and delicious combinations that make great additions to other meals. Plus, their macronutrient content supplements main dishes, sandwiches, and snacks—although they're all also great on their own.

Adding a little heat to garlic, rosemary, and olive oil creates a warm aroma and ideal flavors for roasted potatoes. Paprika adds a zing of extra flavor as well as a splash of color, making a dish that's going to impress guests who smell something delicious when they come over for dinner.

GARLIC & ROSEMARY ROASTED POTATOES

Makes **4** servings | **Serving size** ½ cup cooked | **Prep time** 10 minutes | **Cook time** 1 hour

INGREDIENTS

1½lb (680g) small red or white potatoes, halved or quartered

⅛ cup extra virgin olive oil

1 tsp coarse salt

1 tbsp minced garlic

1 tsp paprika

2 tbsp chopped fresh rosemary leaves

freshly ground black pepper

DIRECTIONS

1 Preheat the oven to 400°F (204°C).

2 In a bowl, combine the potatoes, olive oil, salt, garlic, paprika, and rosemary. Season with pepper and toss until well coated.

3 Spread the potato mixture onto a baking pan and roast until browned and crisp, about 1 hour. Flip periodically to ensure even browning.

4 Remove the potatoes from the oven and serve immediately.

NUTRITION FACTS

per serving

CALORIES

250

TOTAL FAT

11g

TOTAL CARBS

40g

PROTEIN

5g

SALADS & SIDES

MASHED SWEET POTATOES

Makes **4** servings | **Serving size** ⅔ cup | **Prep time** 10 minutes | **Cook time** 30 minutes

Mashing sweet potatoes brings more beta carotene and fiber to this modified classic. Sweet potatoes are also a great source of carbs. Adding coconut milk for creaminess and agave for sweetness makes this dish feel and taste like a savory—but low-calorie—dessert.

INGREDIENTS

4 large sweet potatoes, peeled and quartered

½ cup low-fat organic coconut milk

½ cup unsalted butter

½ cup agave

2 tsp ground cinnamon

DIRECTIONS

1 Fill a large pot three-fourths full with water. Place the pot on the stovetop over high heat and bring the water to a boil. Add the potatoes and cook until tender, about 20 to 30 minutes.

2 With an electric mixer on low, blend the potatoes, slowly adding the coconut milk 1 tablespoon at a time. (Use more or less milk to achieve your desired texture. You can also use an immersion blender.) Add the butter and agave and blend until smooth.

3 Transfer the potatoes to a serving bowl, sprinkle the cinnamon over the top, and serve immediately.

NUTRITION FACTS
per serving

CALORIES
100

TOTAL FAT
4 g

TOTAL CARBS
20 g

PROTEIN
2 g

CHANGE IT UP
Add a dash (or more) of chili powder, ground cayenne pepper, or nutmeg.

Butternut squash's name isn't a misnomer—it's buttery, nutty, and savory. Butternut squash is also loaded with vitamins C and E and potassium. Add aromatic garlic, fresh parsley, and the texture of Parmesan and you have a side that complements nearly any meal.

GARLICKY BUTTERNUT SQUASH

Makes	6 servings	Serving size	¾ cup cooked	Prep time	10 minutes	Cook time	45 to 50 minutes

INGREDIENTS

2 tbsp extra virgin olive oil

2 tbsp minced fresh garlic

3lb (1.4kg) butternut squash, peeled and cut into 1-inch (2.5cm) cubes

sea salt and freshly ground black pepper

⅓ cup grated Parmesan cheese

2 tbsp minced fresh parsley

DIRECTIONS

1 Preheat the oven to 400°F (204°C).

2 In a bowl, combine the olive oil and garlic. Add the squash, season with salt and pepper, and toss to coat.

3 Transfer the squash to an ungreased baking dish and bake uncovered for 45 to 50 minutes.

4 Remove the squash from the oven, sprinkle the cheese and parsley over the top, and serve immediately.

NUTRITION FACTS

per serving

CALORIES

110

TOTAL FAT
6 g

TOTAL CARBS
15 g

PROTEIN
1 g

SALADS & SIDES

GRILLED BALSAMIC ASPARAGUS

Makes 4 to 5 servings | **Serving size** 5 or 6 spears | **Prep time** 5 minutes | **Cook time** 8 to 10 minutes

INGREDIENTS

2 bundles of asparagus

2 tbsp extra virgin olive oil

2 tbsp balsamic vinegar

2 garlic cloves, minced

sea salt and cracked black pepper

1 tsp red pepper flakes

DIRECTIONS

1 Preheat the grill to medium.

2 Cut off the bases of the asparagus spears and place in a quart-sized freezer bag. Add the olive oil, vinegar, and garlic, tossing to evenly coat.

3 Place the spears on the grill and cook until they have distinct grill marks, about 2 to 3 minutes per side.

4 Remove the spears from the grill. Season with salt, pepper, and red pepper flakes. Serve immediately.

This simple side can accompany any meal—from steaks to fish to burgers. Asparagus is a natural diuretic, making this a great way to shed excess water weight. Asparagus is also a low-calorie micronutrient powerhouse that's loaded with antioxidants, folic acid, vitamin K, and vitamin E.

NUTRITION FACTS

per serving

CALORIES

65

TOTAL FAT

4 g

TOTAL CARBS

5 g

PROTEIN

3 g

This powerful combination of ancient grains provides complex carbs, fiber, and healthy fats. Pomegranate seeds are highly touted for their ability to help increase blood flow and aid workouts and recovery. And the zesty citrus dressing pairs wonderfully with the grains.

NUTRITION FACTS

per serving

CALORIES

500

TOTAL FAT

30g

TOTAL CARBS

55g

PROTEIN

11g

ANCIENT GRAINS SALAD
WITH SWEET MUSTARD DRESSING

Makes	3 servings	**Serving size**	1 ¼ cup	**Prep time**	10 minutes	**Cook time**	none

INGREDIENTS

1 cup cooked barley

1 cup cooked red quinoa

1 cup cooked faro

¼ cup toasted chopped walnuts

¼ cup roughly chopped pistachios

¼ cup golden raisins

¼ cup fresh pomegranate seeds

4 scallions, thinly sliced

¼ large red onion, minced

2 celery stalks, finely diced

4 cups mesclun greens

4 radicchio leaves, chopped

1 medium avocado, cubed

for the dressing

½ cup extra virgin olive oil

5 tbsp red wine vinegar

1 tsp sweet mustard

salt and freshly ground black pepper

DIRECTIONS

1 In a bowl, combine all the ingredients except the mesclun greens, radicchio, and avocado.

2 In a bowl, make the dressing by whisking together the olive oil, vinegar, and mustard. Season with salt and pepper. Drizzle just enough dressing over the ingredients to moisten them. (Cover and refrigerate the remaining dressing until ready to serve the salad.)

3 Top the salad with the mesclun greens, radicchio, and avocado. Drizzle the remaining dressing over the top and serve immediately.

Habanero is one of the hottest peppers in the world. This spicy yet refreshingly sweet recipe makes a perfect addition to an outdoor BBQ or a complement to any kind of roasted meat. The honey and the lemon help manage the heat but won't distract from the sharp flavors.

NUTRITION FACTS

per serving

CALORIES

170

TOTAL FAT

10g

TOTAL CARBS

19g

PROTEIN

1g

HABANERO COLESLAW

| Makes | 4 servings | Serving size | ½ cup | Prep time | 15 minutes | Cook time | none |

INGREDIENTS

1 small head of napa cabbage, shredded
1 large carrot, julienned
4 scallions, chopped
salt

for the dressing
1 habanero, seeds removed and flesh minced

1 small garlic clove, minced
pinch of salt
2 tbsp freshly squeezed lemon juice
1 tsp honey
1 tbsp cumin
4 tbsp extra virgin olive oil

DIRECTIONS

1 In a bowl, make the dressing by combining the habanero, garlic, and salt. Use a fork to mash them together to form a paste.

2 Add the lemon juice, honey, and cumin, continuing to mix with a fork. Whisk in the olive oil in a slow stream.

3 In a separate bowl, combine the cabbage, carrot, and scallions. Drizzle the dressing over the coleslaw and gently toss to combine. Season with salt and refrigerate for at least 1 hour before serving.

CHANGE IT UP
You can use a jalapeño instead of a habanero or eliminate the pepper entirely.

SPICY ZOODLES

Makes 4 servings | *Serving size* 1 cup | *Prep time* 8 minutes | *Cook time* 12 minutes

INGREDIENTS

4 medium zucchinis, trimmed

3 tbsp extra virgin olive oil

1 tbsp minced garlic

½ tsp red pepper flakes

2 medium tomatoes, chopped

1 cup fresh basil leaves, torn into pieces

½ cup shredded Parmesan cheese, plus extra

1 tsp cornstarch

2 tsp cold water

salt

DIRECTIONS

1 Use a spiralizer to cut the zucchinis into noodles about the length of spaghetti. Set aside.

2 In a deep skillet on the stovetop over medium heat, heat the olive oil until shimmering. Add the garlic and red pepper flakes, stirring to coat.

3 When the oil begins to bubble around the garlic, add the zucchinis. Toss the noodles continuously with tongs, ensuring they all have a chance to hit the bottom of the skillet. Cook until al dente, about 5 to 7 minutes. (They should be wilted but still have a crunch. Cooking the zucchinis longer than this will turn them mushy.)

4 Stir in the tomatoes, basil, and ½ cup of cheese and cook for 1 minute more. Use tongs to transfer the noodles, tomatoes, and basil to a serving bowl. Leave the liquid in the skillet and bring to a simmer.

5 In a bowl, combine the cornstarch and water. Whisk this mixture into the liquid. Cook until the liquid thickens to a sauce, about 1 minute, whisking continuously. Taste the sauce and season with salt as needed.

6 Drizzle the sauce over the noodles, tomatoes, and basil. Sprinkle extra cheese over the top and serve immediately.

CHANGE IT UP

Eliminate the cheese and cornstarch for a leaner and lower-calorie dish.

I make this dish on low-carb days with lighter training loads or I place my protein on top. This is light and refreshing, with great flavor, making it a superb addition to many dishes. The garlic, tomatoes, and basil give this dish an Italian zing to complement other Italian-inspired entrées.

NUTRITION FACTS

per serving

CALORIES

180

TOTAL FAT

14 g

TOTAL CARBS

10 g

PROTEIN

7 g

Although this dish is low in carbs, it's not low in flavor. It offers plenty of protein and fat for anyone moving toward a keto lifestyle. Crispy Brussels sprouts, gooey cheese, and crunchy speck make this a savory and salty side that pairs well with steak, pork, or fatty fish, like salmon.

BALSAMIC-GLAZED BRUSSELS SPROUTS
WITH GORGONZOLA & SPECK HAM

Makes	4 servings	Serving size	½ to ¾ cup	Prep time	10 minutes	Cook time	50 minutes

INGREDIENTS

1 lb (450g) Brussels sprouts, rinsed and sliced horizontally

2 tbsp extra virgin olive oil

2 tbsp crumbled Gorgonzola cheese

¾ cup diced speck ham

¼ cup balsamic vinegar

salt and freshly ground black pepper

DIRECTIONS

1 Preheat the oven to 400°F (204°C).

2 In a bowl, combine the Brussels sprouts and olive oil. Season with salt and pepper, tossing to coat, and add the cheese and ham.

3 Place the Brussels sprouts mixture on a baking pan and roast until the Brussels sprouts begin to lightly crisp, about 40 minutes.

4 In a saucepan on the stovetop over medium heat, cook the vinegar until it thickens, about 10 minutes, stirring constantly.

5 Remove the Brussels sprouts from the oven, drizzle the balsamic glaze over the top, and serve immediately.

NUTRITION FACTS

per serving

CALORIES

240

TOTAL FAT

17g

TOTAL CARBS

10g

PROTEIN

14g

CHANGE IT UP
Replace the speck ham with pork bacon for a different flavor profile.

SALADS & SIDES

YUCCA FRIES

Makes 6 to 8 servings | *Serving size* 5 to 6 fries | *Prep time* 15 minutes | *Cook time* 30 minutes

INGREDIENTS

2lb (1kg) yucca, peeled and cut into fry shapes

sea salt, divided

2qt (2l) vegetable oil (or canola oil)

finely chopped fresh parsley

DIRECTIONS

1 Place the yucca in a bowl, cover with water, and season with salt. Soak for 10 minutes and drain the water.

2 Fill a large pot three-fourths full with water. Place the pot on the stovetop over high heat and bring the water to a boil. Add the yucca and boil for 15 minutes.

3 Pour the yucca into a strainer and pat dry with paper towels. (The drier the yucca, the crispier the fries.)

4 In a separate deep pot on the stovetop over high heat, heat the vegetable oil until the oil pops if you sprinkle a few drops of water into the oil. Gently add the yucca—be careful not to spray the hot oil—and cook until golden and crispy, about 5 minutes, stirring occasionally.

5 Remove the yucca from the pot and place on paper towels to absorb the excess oil. Transfer the yucca to a bowl, season with salt and parsley, and toss thoroughly. Serve immediately.

Yucca has become my go-to starch in recent years. This versatile tuber provides fast digestion and readily available energy. These fries are great additions to beef and chicken dishes—and kids will love them. Yucca has a meaty flesh, a mild flavor, and an almost nutty taste.

NUTRITION FACTS

per serving

CALORIES

150

TOTAL FAT

9g

TOTAL CARBS

20g

PROTEIN

1g

CHANGE IT UP
Bake the fries at 450°F (232°C) for 25 to 30 minutes for a lower-fat option.

Cauliflower offers a tasty alternative to sugar-laden simple carbohydrate sources. This is a more classic approach that includes turmeric, the powerhouse superfood. This spice has amazing cancer-fighting, anti-inflammatory, and antioxidant properties.

NUTRITION FACTS

per serving

CALORIES

200

TOTAL FAT

14g

TOTAL CARBS

16g

PROTEIN

8g

TURMERIC-DUSTED CAULIFLOWER

Makes 4 servings | Serving size ½ cup cooked | Prep time 5 minutes | Cook time 27 minutes

INGREDIENTS

1 head of cauliflower, cut into 1-inch (2.5cm) florets

3 garlic cloves, minced

¼ cup extra virgin olive oil

1 tsp turmeric

1 tsp ground cumin

¼ tsp red pepper flakes

pinch of kosher salt

DIRECTIONS

1 Preheat the oven to 450°F (232°C).

2 In a bowl, combine the florets, garlic, and olive oil, tossing to coat.

3 In a separate bowl, combine the turmeric, cumin, red pepper flakes, and salt. Sprinkle the turmeric mixture over the cauliflower and toss to coat.

4 Place the cauliflower on a baking pan and cook until browned and tender, about 23 to 27 minutes, turning occasionally.

5 Remove the cauliflower from the oven and serve immediately.

SALADS & SIDES

With just four simple ingredients and a short cooking time, this is a great way to get several micronutrients into your diet, including vitamins C and K, folate (folic acid), potassium, and fiber. In fact, vitamin C has been shown to reduce muscle soreness after intense exercise.

NUTRITION FACTS

per serving

CALORIES

161

TOTAL FAT

14g

TOTAL CARBS

9g

PROTEIN

3g

CHARRED BROCCOLI

Makes	4 servings	Serving size	5 to 8 spears	Prep time	5 minutes	Cook time	10 minutes

INGREDIENTS

1 large head of broccoli

3 tbsp extra virgin olive oil

sea salt and freshly ground black pepper

DIRECTIONS

1 Preheat the oven to 425°F (218°C).

2 Thoroughly wash and dry the broccoli. (The drier the broccoli, the more it will crisp.) Cut into medium-sized spears and coat well with olive oil.

3 Spread the spears on a baking pan and season with salt and pepper. Bake for 10 minutes, flip, and bake for another 10 minutes.

4 Remove the broccoli from the oven and serve immediately.

CHANGE IT UP
Add red pepper flakes, nutritional yeast, garlic salt, and/or dill for extra flavor.

BROCCOLINI & PINE NUTS

Makes 2 servings | **Serving size** 3oz (85g) | **Prep time** 2 minutes | **Cook time** 15 minutes

INGREDIENTS

6oz (170g) broccolini

2 tsp extra virgin olive oil

pinch of red pepper flakes

sea salt and freshly ground black pepper

2 small garlic cloves, minced

1 tbsp pine nuts

1 tbsp shredded Parmesan cheese

DIRECTIONS

1 Preheat the oven to 400°F (204°C). Spray a baking dish with nonstick cooking spray.

2 In a bowl, combine the broccolini, olive oil, and red pepper flakes. Season with salt and pepper, tossing to coat. Place the broccolini in the baking dish and roast until fork tender, about 10 to 12 minutes.

3 Remove the dish from the oven and add the garlic, gently mixing to coat. Place the dish back into the oven and cook for 2 minutes more.

4 In a frying pan on the stovetop over medium heat, toast the pine nuts until golden, about 3 minutes, stirring frequently or shaking the pan. (Keep an eye on the pan at all times. Don't let the nuts be stationary for too long. Otherwise, they'll toast unevenly and might burn.)

5 Remove the broccolini from the oven, sprinkle the pine nuts and cheese over the top, and serve immediately.

Broccolini is a hybrid of broccoli and gai lan (Chinese broccoli) that looks and tastes a little like asparagus despite not being related to that veggie. Pine nuts have a nutty and almost buttery texture, which pairs brilliantly with the bitter and somewhat sweet flavor of the broccolini.

NUTRITION FACTS

per serving

CALORIES

105

TOTAL FAT

8g

TOTAL CARBS

4g

PROTEIN

3g

SALADS & SIDES

Almost everyone loves mashed potatoes, but it doesn't always fit into your personal or training diet. This recipe is super easy to make and is a great and healthy alternative to high-fat mashed potatoes. This side also comes in handy when you need to keep your carb intake low.

CAULIFLOWER MASH

Makes	4 servings	Serving size	¾ cup	Prep time	10 minutes	Cook time	10 minutes

INGREDIENTS

1 medium head of cauliflower, trimmed and cut into small florets

1 tbsp extra virgin olive oil

salt and freshly ground black pepper

DIRECTIONS

1 Fill a large pot three-fourths full with water. Place the pot on the stovetop over high heat and bring the water to a boil. Add the cauliflower and cook until tender, about 10 minutes.

2 Drain all but ¼ cup of the cooking liquid and transfer the cauliflower to a food processor. Add the olive oil and reserved water 1 tablespoon at a time and purée until smooth. (You can use a potato masher instead.)

3 Transfer the cauliflower mash to a serving bowl, season with salt and pepper, and serve immediately.

NUTRITION FACTS

per serving

CALORIES

110

TOTAL FAT

9g

TOTAL CARBS

8g

PROTEIN

3g

SMASHED PEAS & FETA

Makes 2 servings | *Serving size* ½ cup | *Prep time* 35 minutes | *Cook time* 5 minutes

INGREDIENTS

½ cup feta cheese

2 tsp extra virgin olive oil, divided

1 tsp chopped fresh thyme leaves

¼ tsp red pepper flakes

grated zest and juice of 1 lemon

1 cup shelled fresh or frozen peas

freshly ground black pepper

DIRECTIONS

1 Into a bowl, crumble the feta into large pieces and add 1 teaspoon of olive oil, thyme, red pepper flakes, and lemon zest. Stir gently to combine and let rest for 30 minutes.

2 Fill a small saucepan half full with water. Place the saucepan on the stovetop over medium heat and bring the water to a boil. Add the peas and cook until tender, about 5 minutes.

3 Drain the peas and transfer to a food processor. Add the lemon juice and the remaining 1 teaspoon of olive oil. Pulse into a chunky mash.

4 Transfer the mashed peas to a serving bowl and stir in the feta mixture. Season with pepper and serve immediately.

This warm and slightly salty treat makes a great side dish or it can also work as an appealing appetizer. Peas are a surprising source of vegetarian protein, and combining them with high-quality protein found in feta, this dish provides a significant 9 grams of protein per ½ cup.

NUTRITION FACTS

per serving

CALORIES

180

TOTAL FAT

12 g

TOTAL CARBS

11 g

PROTEIN

9 g

SALADS & SIDES

CA stands for Chris Algieri, not California, although some of the flavors might have a West Coast feel to them. Different textures make this as fun to eat as it is to make. From the crispy bacon to the savory avocado to the bite of the blue cheese, this will become a favorite protein-packed salad.

NUTRITION FACTS

per serving

CALORIES

350

TOTAL FAT

30g

TOTAL CARBS

8g

PROTEIN

15g

CA TURKEY COBB SALAD

| Makes | 4 servings | Serving size | 4oz to 6oz (110g to 170g) | Prep time | 15 minutes | Cook time | none |

INGREDIENTS

2 cups chopped romaine

4 hard-boiled eggs, peeled and quartered

8 slices turkey bacon, cooked and crumbled

1 medium avocado, quartered and diced

4oz (110g) blue cheese

5oz (140g) cherry tomatoes, halved

½ cup alfalfa sprouts

1 tbsp chopped chives

kosher salt and freshly ground black pepper

for the dressing

⅓ cup red wine vinegar

1 tbsp Dijon mustard

⅔ cup extra virgin olive oil

kosher salt and freshly ground black pepper

DIRECTIONS

1 In a 16-ounce (450-gram) Mason jar, make the dressing by combining the vinegar, mustard, and olive oil. Season with salt and pepper and set aside.

2 On a platter, spread out the romaine and add rows of eggs, bacon, avocado, blue cheese, tomatoes, and sprouts across the lettuce.

3 Sprinkle the chives over the top, drizzle the dressing over the top, and season with salt and pepper. Serve immediately.

Bursting with healthy fats, dark, leafy greens, protein-laden dairy, and heart-healthy seafood, this salad is a great choice for helping you look like a fighter. This is why Mediterranean cuisine is one of the healthiest. Serve this as an appetizer or a side or use it as a base to your favorite protein dish.

NUTRITION FACTS

per serving

CALORIES

TOTAL FAT

TOTAL CARBS

PROTEIN

GREEK SALAD
WITH RED WINE DRESSING

Makes	3 servings	Serving size	2 cups	Prep time	20 minutes	Cook time	none

INGREDIENTS

1 head of romaine, chopped
1 medium red onion, thinly sliced
6oz (170g) pitted black olives
1 green bell pepper, chopped
1 red bell pepper, chopped
2 large Roma tomatoes, chopped
1 medium cucumber, sliced
1 cup crumbled feta cheese

for the dressing

6 tbsp extra virgin olive oil
3 tbsp red wine vinegar
1 tsp dried oregano
juice of 1 lemon
freshly ground black pepper

DIRECTIONS

1 In a bowl, combine the romaine, onion, olives, bell peppers, tomatoes, cucumber, and feta.

2 In a separate bowl, make the dressing by whisking together the olive oil, vinegar, oregano, and lemon juice. Season with pepper.

3 Drizzle the dressing over the salad, toss to coat, and serve immediately.

CHANGE IT UP
Pair this with Grilled Chicken Gyro (p. 78) and Homemade Hummus (p. 116) for an all-Greek meal.

GRANDPA'S TOMATO & CUCUMBER SALAD

Makes 4 to 5 servings | *Serving size* 3oz to 4oz (85g to 110g) | *Prep time* 5 minutes | *Cook time* none

As far back as I can remember, my grandfather used to make this simple salad fresh from his garden each and every day during the summer months. I have fond memories of watching him assemble and enjoy this salad. And I'm excited to share this experience and recipe with you.

INGREDIENTS

8oz (225g) cherry tomatoes, halved or quartered

1 large seedless cucumber, sliced and quartered

¼ medium red onion, thinly sliced

1 tsp finely chopped fresh oregano

2 tbsp extra virgin olive oil

1 tbsp red wine vinegar

salt and freshly ground black pepper

DIRECTIONS

1 In a serving bowl, combine the tomatoes, cucumber, onion, and oregano. Drizzle the olive oil and vinegar over the top, gently tossing to coat and evenly distribute the ingredients.

2 Cover and refrigerate until ready to serve. Season with salt and pepper before serving.

NUTRITION FACTS

per serving

CALORIES
115

TOTAL FAT
10g

TOTAL CARBS
8g

PROTEIN
1g

CHANGE IT UP
Add feta (or another favorite cheese) or a few diced pepperoncini for some added salty and spicy flavors.

This is a summer staple of mine that features crisp kale, "meaty" Great Northern white beans, crunchy trail mix, and a savory poppy seed dressing! It's great to eat on a summer day and it's also super versatile—complex enough for a standalone meal or as side dish to accompany your plate.

NUTRITION FACTS

per serving

CALORIES

350

TOTAL FAT

20g

TOTAL CARBS

25g

PROTEIN

10g

SUMMERTIME KALE SALAD
WITH TANGY POPPY SEED DRESSING

| **Makes** 2 servings | **Serving size** 1¼ cup | **Prep time** 15 minutes | **Cook time** 20 minutes |

INGREDIENTS

¾ cup cauliflower, coarsely chopped

salt and freshly ground black pepper

2 cups kale, chopped into ½-inch (1.25cm) strips

⅓ cup goat cheese

½ cup Great Northern white beans

½ cup trail mix

for the dressing

½ cup vegetable oil (or light olive oil)

¼ cup red wine vinegar

¼ cup granulated sugar

1 tsp poppy seeds

1 tsp dried mustard

1 tsp salt

DIRECTIONS

1 Preheat the oven to 450°F (232°C).

2 Place the cauliflower on a baking pan, season with salt and pepper, and roast until golden and tender, about 20 minutes. Chop and set aside.

3 In a 16-ounce (450-gram) Mason jar, make the dressing by combining all the ingredients. Put the lid on tightly and shake the jar well.

4 In a bowl, combine the cauliflower, kale, cheese, beans, and trail mix. Drizzle the dressing over the top, tossing to coat, and serve immediately.

CHANGE IT UP
Add roasted chicken breast (or another protein of choice) and avocado to make this salad a more complete meal.

BROCCOLI & CHICKPEA SALAD

My sister-in-law Stephane stumbled upon this recipe after mixing leftovers into the same Tupperware container. I created the dressing to add to this delicious and nutritious side, which is loaded with good fats and healthy fiber, plus a strong hit of protein (6 grams per serving).

Makes 4 servings | **Serving size** 1 ¼ cup | **Prep time** 5 minutes | **Cook time** 9 minutes

INGREDIENTS

4 cups broccoli florets

15oz (420g) chickpeas, drained and rinsed

½ cup chopped fresh parsley

for the dressing

2 garlic cloves, minced

2 scallions, chopped

2 tsp Dijon mustard

¼ cup freshly squeezed lemon juice

5 tbsp extra virgin olive oil

kosher salt and freshly ground black pepper

DIRECTIONS

1 Preheat the oven to broil.

2 In a pot on the stovetop over medium heat, bring 1 inch (2.5cm) of water to a boil. Place a steamer basket over the pot and place the broccoli in the basket. Cover the pot and steam the broccoli until tender to the bite, about 3 minutes for crisp-tender florets and up to 8 minutes for fully tender.

3 Remove the broccoli from the steamer and set aside to cool.

4 Chop the broccoli into bite-sized pieces, place in a bowl, and add the chickpeas and parsley.

5 In a separate bowl, make the dressing by combining the garlic, scallions, mustard, and lemon juice. Slowly whisk in the olive oil and season with salt and pepper.

6 Drizzle the dressing over the broccoli and chickpea mixture, tossing until evenly distributed. Place the broccoli mixture on a baking pan and broil until lightly browned and crispy, about 1 to 2 minutes.

7 Remove the salad from the oven and serve immediately.

NUTRITION FACTS

per serving

CALORIES

TOTAL FAT

TOTAL CARBS

PROTEIN

SALADS & SIDES

I've always been partial to the Mediterranean diet because it's heavy on dark, leafy greens, proteins from the sea, colorful vegetables, and healthy fats. Hummus is a great complement to this diet. Put this spread on sandwiches or enjoy it with crackers, bread, or fresh veggies.

HOMEMADE HUMMUS

Makes 6 to 7 servings | **Serving size** ¼ cup | **Prep time** 10 minutes | **Cook time** none

INGREDIENTS

15oz (420g) chickpeas, including aquafaba liquid

2 garlic cloves, chopped

2 tbsp tahini (optional)

¼ cup extra virgin olive oil, plus extra

2 tbsp freshly squeezed lemon juice

1 tsp cumin

½ tsp sea salt

¼ tsp paprika

chopped fresh parsley

DIRECTIONS

1 In a food processor, combine the chickpeas (reserving the liquid), garlic, tahini (if using), olive oil, lemon juice, cumin, and salt. Add the reserved aquafaba in a steady stream and purée until smooth and creamy. (Add 1 to 2 tablespoons of water to achieve your desired consistency.)

2 Transfer the hummus to a bowl, drizzle a little olive oil over the top, and sprinkle the paprika and parsley over the top before serving. (Refrigerated hummus in a covered container will last 3 to 5 days. Hummus will last for 6 months in the freezer.)

NUTRITION FACTS

per serving

CALORIES

100

TOTAL FAT

5g

TOTAL CARBS

12g

PROTEIN

3g

SALADS & SIDES

PREP TIP *I like my hummus to be extra garlicky to the point of almost being spicy. Add more or less garlic to your liking.*

SANDWICHES & SNACKS

Whether you're between meals or need to nibble on something before a meal, these recipes will help squelch your hunger pains. You might even find some of them to be good replacements for a meal now and again. But when you need a boost of energy or a quick meal with a more well-rounded nutritional impact, these dishes can help.

Canned tuna has long been one of my favorite lean protein sources because of its ease of preparation, versatility, and price. This simple recipe is the kind of dish I could make and eat every day—and some training weeks, I certainly do. Now you can also enjoy it anytime you want.

OPEN-FACED TUNA MELT

| Makes | 1 serving | Serving size | 1 sandwich | Prep time | 8 minutes | Cook time | 2 minutes |

INGREDIENTS

3oz (85g) chunk light tuna, drained

1½ tbsp mayonnaise

2 tsp Dijon mustard

salt and freshly ground black pepper

1 slice whole-grain bread

2 thick-cut tomato slices

1 slice provolone cheese

DIRECTIONS

1 Preheat the oven to broil.

2 In a bowl, combine the tuna, mayonnaise, and mustard. Season with salt and pepper.

3 Place the tuna mixture on the bread, top with tomato slices and cheese, and broil until the cheese melts, about 1 to 2 minutes.

4 Remove the melt from the oven and serve immediately.

NUTRITION FACTS

per serving

CALORIES

350

TOTAL FAT

23g

TOTAL CARBS

21g

PROTEIN

26g

SANDWICHES & SNACKS

PREP TIP *Try to avoid white albacore tuna to limit your mercury exposure.*

CHANGE IT UP
You can replace the bread with a whole-wheat roll.

AVOCADO TWIST TUNA SALAD

Makes 1 serving | **Serving size** ⅔ cup | **Prep time** 5 minutes | **Cook time** none

INGREDIENTS

5oz (140g) chunk light tuna, drained

½ medium avocado

2 tbsp Dijon mustard

1 tsp paprika

1 tsp pink Himalayan sea salt

1 tsp ground black pepper

DIRECTIONS

1 In a bowl, mash together the tuna, avocado, and mustard.

2 Transfer the tuna salad to a serving bowl. Sprinkle the paprika, salt, and pepper over the top. Serve immediately.

This is a quick go-to sandwich if you're not a fan of mayo, you're a pescatarian, or you need to limit saturated fats. You're essentially swapping out mayonnaise for avocado, but eat this quickly because avocado oxidizes rapidly. This is great on toast, in wraps or salads, or with chips or crackers.

NUTRITION FACTS

per serving

CALORIES

325

TOTAL FAT

22g

TOTAL CARBS

6g

PROTEIN

26g

My friend Tobin is an avid fisherman in south Florida and he'll often bring me fresh-caught tuna. There's nothing like fresh tuna and a creamy and spicy dressing rolled up perfectly into a wrap for lunch. Various veggies bring some crunch and plenty of micronutrients.

TOBIN'S SEARED TUNA WRAPS

Makes	2 wraps	Serving size	1 wrap	Prep time	10 minutes	Cook time	10 minutes

NUTRITION FACTS

per serving

CALORIES
400

TOTAL FAT
15g

TOTAL CARBS
45g

PROTEIN
28g

INGREDIENTS

10oz (285g) ahi tuna steak

salt and freshly ground black pepper

1 tbsp sesame seeds, divided

1 tsp extra virgin olive oil

2 tsp sesame oil, divided

¼ cup organic mayonnaise

1 tsp soy sauce

¾ tsp sriracha

2 burrito-sized whole-wheat flour tortillas

2 cups mixed greens

1 cup shredded carrots

1 cup shredded cabbage

½ medium avocado, sliced thinly

DIRECTIONS

1 Dry the tuna with paper towels and season with salt and pepper. Sprinkle ½ tablespoon of sesame seeds evenly on both sides.

2 In a frying pan on the stovetop over medium-high heat, heat the olive oil and 1 teaspoon of sesame oil until shimmering. Add the tuna, sear for 45 seconds, flip, and sear for 45 seconds more. Remove the pan from the stovetop and allow the tuna to cool slightly.

3 In a bowl, whisk together the mayonnaise, soy sauce, sriracha, and the remaining 1 teaspoon of sesame oil.

4 Slice the tuna into ¼-inch (.5cm) pieces. Spread an equal amount of the mayonnaise mixture on each tortilla. Spread an equal amount of mixed greens on each tortilla. Place half the carrots down the middle of each tortilla and place half the cabbage on top of the carrots. Place an equal amount of tuna, avocado, and the remaining ½ tablespoon of sesame seeds on top of each tortilla.

5 Wrap the tortillas like burritos, cut in half, and serve immediately.

CALIFORNIA FISH TACOS

Makes 4 tacos | **Serving size** 2 tacos | **Prep time** 30 minutes | **Cook time** 10 minutes

I picked up this recipe while at training camp on the West Coast. I was boxing out of Oxnard, California, and I'd take weekend trips down the Pacific Coast Highway to Malibu. Fish tacos there were out of this world, and I've recreated them so you can enjoy them wherever you are.

INGREDIENTS

4 boneless fish fillets, 1-inch (2.5cm) thick (mahi-mahi or cod)

salt and freshly ground black pepper

1 tbsp extra virgin olive oil

8 small corn tortillas

1 cup shredded red cabbage

½ cup pico de gallo

1 medium avocado, cut into 16 slices

¼ cup sour cream

2 limes

DIRECTIONS

1 Preheat the grill to medium and spray with nonstick cooking spray.

2 Place the fillets on the grill and season with salt and pepper. Cover the grill and cook the fish until the flesh pulls away from the grill grates, about 4 minutes. Brush with the olive oil, flip, and season with salt and pepper. Cook for 4 minutes more. Remove the fish from the grill and set aside.

3 Warm the tortillas on the grill until softened, about 20 to 30 seconds.

4 Place half a fillet on each tortilla and top each fillet with equal amounts of cabbage, pico de gallo, avocado, and sour cream. (Add sliced limes to the tacos or quarter them to serve on the side.) Serve immediately.

CHANGE IT UP
Try this with breaded cod (baked or fried), grilled cod, or mahi-mahi (grilled or fried).

NUTRITION FACTS

per serving

CALORIES

280

TOTAL FAT

10g

TOTAL CARBS

28g

PROTEIN

24g

Because of low calories and low carbs, this is a great late-night snack. It also has the thermogenic effect of capsaicin, which can help fire up your metabolism. Capscasin is the active compound in chili peppers that can reduce appetite, lower blood pressure, and combat obesity.

NUTRITION FACTS

per serving

CALORIES

65

TOTAL FAT

4 g

TOTAL CARBS

6 g

PROTEIN

1 g

CHILI-DUSTED POPCORN

Makes 4 to 5 servings | **Serving size** 2 cups | **Prep time** 5 minutes | **Cook time** 7 minutes

INGREDIENTS

⅛ tsp chili powder
⅛ tsp ground cayenne pepper
1 tbsp garlic salt
2 tbsp nutritional yeast
½ tsp sea salt

⅛ tsp ground black pepper
1 bag all-natural, low-fat, low-sodium cooked popcorn
1½ tbsp canola oil

DIRECTIONS

1 In a bowl, combine the chili powder, cayenne, garlic salt, nutritional yeast, sea salt, and pepper.

2 In a separate bowl, combine the popcorn and oil, tossing to coat. Sprinkle the spice mixture over the top, toss again, and serve immediately.

PREP TIP // *You can also make the popcorn yourself rather than buying prepared popcorn.*

I love one-dish snacks that contain protein, carbs, and fats. You can make this with ground turkey, bison, or lamb or vegetarian style with beans or chunks of tofu or tempeh. And orange, red, and yellow peppers impart more phytonutrients and antioxidants than green peppers.

NUTRITION FACTS

per serving

CALORIES

350

TOTAL FAT

15g

TOTAL CARBS

29g

PROTEIN

29g

BAKED STUFFED PEPPERS

Makes	4 servings	Serving size	1 pepper	Prep time	15 minutes	Cook time	40 minutes

INGREDIENTS

4 large bell peppers (any color)

1lb (450g) lean ground beef (85%)

2 tbsp chopped white onion

1 cup cooked rice

1 tsp salt

2 garlic cloves, finely chopped

2 cups organic tomato sauce, divided

3oz (85g) shredded sharp Cheddar cheese

DIRECTIONS

1 Preheat the oven to 350°F (177°C).

2 Cut the tops off the peppers, remove the seeds and membranes, and rinse the peppers. Add enough water to a 4-quart (4-liter) Dutch oven to cover the peppers. Place the Dutch oven on the stovetop over high heat, bring the water to a boil, and add the peppers. Cook for 2 minutes, remove the peppers from the Dutch oven, and set aside.

3 In a skillet on the stovetop over medium heat, cook the beef and onion until the beef browns, about 8 to 10 minutes, stirring occasionally. Stir in the rice, salt, garlic, and 1 cup of tomato sauce and cook until hot, about 1 to 2 minutes.

4 Stuff the peppers with the beef mixture. Stand the peppers upright in an ungreased square glass baking dish and pour the remaining 1 cup of tomato sauce over the peppers.

5 Cover the dish tightly with aluminum foil and bake for 10 minutes. Uncover and bake until the peppers are tender, about 15 minutes more.

6 Remove the peppers from the oven, sprinkle the cheese over the top, and serve immediately.

HEIRLOOM TOMATO & AVOCADO FLATBREAD

Makes 1 serving | **Serving size** 2 slices | **Prep time** 10 minutes | **Cook time** 40 minutes

I came up with this recipe when my nephews asked me to make them a pizza. I brought together some of my favorite flavors to make this more than a cheese pizza. This savory and herbaceous treat makes a great appetizer or snack and pairs great with a glass of red wine—but for adults only.

INGREDIENTS

1 tbsp extra virgin olive oil

3 garlic cloves, peeled and sliced lengthwise

1½ pints heirloom tomatoes

5 tbsp avocado oil, divided

2 tbsp chopped fresh rosemary

salt and freshly ground black pepper

1 slice of flatbread

3oz (85g) shredded mozzarella cheese

2 tbsp chopped fresh basil

DIRECTIONS

1 Preheat the oven to 400°F (204°C).

2 In a skillet on the stovetop over medium heat, heat the olive oil until shimmering. Add the garlic and sauté until crispy and lightly browned, about 2 to 3 minutes, stirring frequently. Remove the garlic from the skillet, reserve the oil, and spread the garlic slices on paper towels to dry.

3 In a bowl, toss the garlic and tomatoes with 3 tablespoons of avocado oil and rosemary. Season generously with salt and pepper.

4 Spread the tomato mixture evenly on a baking pan lined with parchment paper. Bake until the tomatoes burst, about 20 to 30 minutes.

5 Place the flatbread on a separate baking pan lined with parchment paper and brush with the remaining 2 tablespoons of avocado oil. Arrange the tomato mixture evenly on the flatbread, sprinkle the cheese over the top, and bake for 5 to 10 minutes.

6 Remove the flatbread from the oven and sprinkle the basil over the top. Cut in half and serve immediately.

NUTRITION FACTS
per serving

CALORIES

360

TOTAL FAT

25 g

TOTAL CARBS

24 g

PROTEIN

15 g

CHANGE IT UP
Replace the avocado oil with extra virgin olive oil.

This is a go-to snack for me and for fighters I work with because it's low in carbs, fats, and calories but high in protein and flavor! Turkey burgers are versatile and not only go great on buns but also on top of salads, chopped up with rice dishes, or as an entrée protein.

NUTRITION FACTS

per serving

CALORIES

206

TOTAL FAT

5g

TOTAL CARBS

9g

PROTEIN

33g

TURKEY BURGER

Makes	4 burgers	Serving size	1 burger	Prep time	5 minutes	Cook time	8 to 10 minutes

INGREDIENTS

1 lb (450g) lean ground turkey (99%)

1 cup chopped baby spinach

½ cup crumbled feta cheese

1 tsp pink Himalayan sea salt

1 tsp white pepper

1 large egg

½ cup fine oat bran or old-fashioned oats

DIRECTIONS

1 Heat the grill to hot.

2 In a bowl, combine all the ingredients. Form the mixture into 4 equal-sized patties and cook until completely cooked through, about 4 minutes per side.

3 Remove the burgers from the grill, place on buns, and add your favorite toppings or place on top of salad greens. Serve immediately.

BISON SLIDERS

Makes 8 sliders | *Serving size* 2 sliders | *Prep time* 30 minutes | *Cook time* 15 minutes

INGREDIENTS

12oz (340g) lean ground bison (85%)

1 large egg

½ cup oat bran

½ cup finely diced white onion

1 tsp finely diced garlic

½ tsp salt

½ tsp ground black pepper

8 cracked wheat slider buns

4 slices sharp Cheddar cheese

1 medium tomato, sliced

1 medium red onion, sliced

4 dill cocktail pickles, sliced

4 tsp ketchup

4 tsp Dijon mustard

DIRECTIONS

1 Preheat the grill to medium.

2 In a bowl, combine the bison, egg, oat bran, onion, garlic, salt, and pepper. Shape the mixture into 8 patties, place on the grill, and cook until still slightly pink in the middle, about 5 minutes per side.

3 Cut each slice of cheese in half and place one on each patty for the last minute of cooking.

4 Remove the patties from the grill and place on buns. Add an equal amount of tomato slices, onion slices, pickle slices, ketchup, and mustard to each. Skewer with cocktail toothpicks and serve immediately.

These sliders are a great way to introduce bison to nonbelievers. People assume bison is gamey, but when it's cooked properly, you can't tell the difference from traditional beef, although your gut will thank you because bison is 30% leaner for the same amount of protein than beef!

NUTRITION FACTS

per serving

CALORIES

400

TOTAL FAT

13g

TOTAL CARBS

34g

PROTEIN

34g

CHANGE IT UP
Try this with venison, which is even leaner than bison.

SANDWICHES & SNACKS

My desire to help my family members eat incredibly nutritious and healthy sardines inspired me to create and perfect this dish. Searing the fish makes them crispy, and combining citrus from the lemon and heat from the red pepper flakes makes this an even more delicious treat.

SARDINE CROSTINI

Makes 4 slices | **Serving size** 2 slices | **Prep time** 5 minutes | **Cook time** 10 minutes

INGREDIENTS

1 tbsp extra virgin olive oil
1 garlic clove, chopped
½ tsp red pepper flakes
grated zest and juice of 1 lemon
240g sardines in oil, drained

1 tbsp chopped fresh parsley
8 endive leaves
4 slices brown bread, toasted
2 tsp capers, divided

DIRECTIONS

1 In a frying pan on the stovetop over high heat, heat the olive oil until shimmering. Add the garlic and red pepper flakes and sauté until the garlic is shiny but not browned, about 2 minutes.

2 Add the lemon zest and sardines and cook until warm, about 3 minutes. Remove the sardines from the stovetop, sprinkle the parsley over the top, and drizzle the lemon juice over the top.

3 Place 2 endive leaves on each slice of bread, add an equal amount of sardines and capers on top of each crostini, and serve immediately.

NUTRITION FACTS

per serving

CALORIES

400

TOTAL FAT

22 g

TOTAL CARBS

30 g

PROTEIN

29 g

SANDWICHES & SNACKS

PERFECT PENNE

Makes 4 servings | *Serving size* 1 to 1½ cups | *Prep time* 15 minutes | *Cook time* 35 minutes

INGREDIENTS

¼ cup extra virgin olive oil

6 garlic cloves, sliced

1 tsp red pepper flakes

28oz (800g) diced tomatoes

½ cup tomato sauce

1 bunch of fresh basil, chopped

4qt (4l) water

1 tsp salt

12oz (340g) uncooked penne

1 cup grape tomatoes, halved

4 tbsp ricotta cheese, divided

8 tbsp grated Parmesan cheese, divided

DIRECTIONS

1 In a skillet on the stovetop over medium heat, heat the olive oil until shimmering. Add the garlic and sauté for 3 minutes. Add the red pepper flakes and sauté for 1 minute more.

2 Add the diced tomatoes, tomato sauce, and basil. Simmer for 20 minutes, stirring occasionally.

3 In a pot on the stovetop over medium heat, bring the water and salt to a boil. Add the penne and cook until tender, about 8 minutes.

4 Drain the penne and stir into the sauce. Add the grape tomatoes and simmer for 3 minutes to soak up the flavors.

5 Remove the penne from the stovetop and place an equal amount in 4 bowls. Add 1 tablespoon of ricotta and 2 tablespoons of Parmesan to each bowl. Serve immediately.

Although I'm Italian on my father's side, I'm actually not a big pasta eater. But being an athlete, there are often times where a big carb-centered dish is necessary—and pasta does the trick quite well. Enjoy this penne with a simple red tomato sauce, fresh herbs, and creamy cheese.

NUTRITION FACTS

per serving

CALORIES

240

TOTAL FAT

8g

TOTAL CARBS

31g

PROTEIN

5g

Dark semisweet chocolate combined with dried cherries makes this snack feel like a dessert. With 50 grams of fast-digesting carbs, this is great for a pre-workout boost or a post-workout recharge. But you'll soon find out that it's a great treat for any time of day.

NUTRITION FACTS

per serving

CALORIES

TOTAL FAT

TOTAL CARBS

50g

PROTEIN

DARK CHOCOLATE & CHERRY BARS

| Makes | 4 servings | Serving size | 1 bar | Prep time | 10 minutes | Cook time | 20 to 25 minutes |

INGREDIENTS

1 cup old-fashioned rolled oats

¼ cup dark semisweet chocolate chips

¼ cup chopped dried cherries

1 tsp pure cocoa powder

2 scoops vanilla whey protein powder

⅓ cup unsweetened almond milk

¼ cup honey

1 tbsp almond butter

1 tsp pure vanilla extract

DIRECTIONS

1 Preheat the oven to 350°F (177°C). Spray a baking dish with nonstick cooking spray.

2 In a bowl, combine the oats, chocolate chips, cherries, cocoa powder, and protein powder.

3 In a separate bowl, combine the almond milk, honey, almond butter, and vanilla. Pour the wet ingredients into the dry ingredients and stir well.

4 Pour the mixture into the baking dish and bake until the top browns, about 30 minutes.

5 Remove the oat mixture from the oven, refrigerate for 1 hour, and cut into 4 equal-sized bars before serving. (Refrigerate the bars in a sealed container for up to 6 days.)

CHANGE IT UP
Replace the almond butter with cashew butter for a slightly different flavor.

Complex carbs from the oats and fast-digesting carbs from the bananas make this a midday or between-meals snack. Medium chain triglycerides (MCT), which are found in coconut oil, have been shown to increase your blood's lipid levels of HDL— the "good" cholesterol.

NUTRITION FACTS

per serving

CALORIES

350

TOTAL FAT

20g

TOTAL CARBS

45g

PROTEIN

6g

SANDWICHES & SNACKS

NUTTY BANANA & OAT BARS

Makes	12 servings	Serving size	1 bar	Prep time	15 minutes	Cook time	22 minutes

INGREDIENTS

1 cup mashed bananas (from 2 medium overripe bananas)

½ cup coconut oil, melted

⅔ cup honey

1 large egg, lightly beaten

2 tsp pure vanilla extract

2½ cups rolled oats

1¼ cup whole-wheat pastry flour

½ tsp ground cinnamon

½ tsp salt

¼ cup chopped nuts (such as pecans or walnuts)

DIRECTIONS

1 Move an oven rack to the center position and preheat the oven to 350°F (177°C). Spray a baking dish with nonstick cooking spray.

2 In a bowl, combine the bananas, coconut oil, honey, egg, and vanilla.

3 In a separate bowl, whisk together the oats, pastry, cinnamon, salt, and nuts. Pour the wet ingredients into the dry ingredients and stir well.

4 Pour the batter into the baking dish and ensure the mixture has an even thickness. Bake until the edges begin to turn golden, about 18 to 22 minutes.

5 Remove the mixture from the oven, cool for 10 minutes, and cut into 12 equal-sized bars before serving.

PREP TIP *Store in an airtight container for up to 5 days. Or wrap them in parchment paper and freeze for up to 3 months.*

OATMEAL & PUMPKIN SEED BARS

Makes 4 servings | **Serving size** 1 bar | **Prep time** 10 minutes | **Cook time** 30 minutes

This recipe makes a great travel bar that's low in fat and gives a good protein boost. It's ideal for breakfast, as a snack, as a side item, or for some pre-workout fuel. Pumpkin seeds are a great source of zinc and magnesium, which can help with sleep, immunity, and hormone health.

INGREDIENTS

2 cups old-fashioned rolled oats

¾ cup vanilla whey protein powder

2 tbsp raw pumpkin seeds

1 tsp ground cinnamon

⅓ cup unsweetened almond milk

2 tbsp honey

1 tsp pure vanilla extract

DIRECTIONS

1 Preheat the oven to 350°F (177°C). Spray a baking dish with nonstick cooking spray.

2 In a bowl, combine the oats, protein powder, seeds, and cinnamon.

3 In a separate bowl, combine the almond milk, honey, and vanilla. Pour the wet ingredients into the dry ingredients and stir well to combine.

4 Pour the mixture into the baking dish and bake until the top browns, about 30 minutes.

5 Remove the mixture from the oven, refrigerate for 1 hour, and cut into 4 equal-sized bars before serving.

NUTRITION FACTS

per serving

CALORIES

280

TOTAL FAT

6g

TOTAL CARBS

37g

PROTEIN

22g

This is one of my oldest snacks, which I enjoyed throughout my time in college and graduate school. I used to wrap these in aluminum foil and bring them to class and to the gym every single day. They're loaded with fast-digesting carbs, delicious peanut butter, and crisp green apple.

PEANUT BUTTER & APPLE CRISP

| Makes | 2 servings | Serving size | 1 crisp | Prep time | 5 minutes | Cook time | none |

INGREDIENTS

2 tbsp all-natural peanut butter, divided

2 rice cakes

1 green apple, thinly sliced

2 tsp ground cinnamon, divided

DIRECTIONS

1 Spread 1 tablespoon of peanut butter on each rice cake.

2 Arrange an equal amount of apple slices on top of the peanut butter for each rice cake.

3 Sprinkle 1 teaspoon of cinnamon over the top of each rice cake and serve immediately.

NUTRITION FACTS

per serving

CALORIES

340

TOTAL FAT

16g

TOTAL CARBS

43g

PROTEIN

9g

SANDWICHES & SNACKS

RICE CAKE MADNESS

Makes 1 serving | **Serving size** 2 rice cakes | **Prep time** 5 minutes | **Cook time** none

INGREDIENTS

2 rice cakes

1 tbsp cottage cheese

1 tbsp raspberry jam

1 tbsp puffed quinoa

1 tsp sunflower seeds

1 tbsp almond butter

½ medium banana, sliced

1 tsp chia seeds

1 tsp shaved coconut

DIRECTIONS

1 Place 1 rice cake on a serving plate. Spread the cottage cheese over one half and raspberry jam on the other half. Sprinkle the puffed quinoa and sunflower seeds over the top.

2 Place the other rice cake on a separate serving plate. Spread the almond butter evenly on top. Layer the banana slices down the middle and top one side with chia seeds and the other with coconut. Serve the rice cakes immediately.

Before bed the night before my fights in kickboxing and boxing, I eat this for a snack. It's also great for hydration and fueling energy stores before exercise. Carbs from the rice cakes and fruit, fats from the nut butter, and protein from the cottage cheese make this a great boost.

NUTRITION FACTS

per serving

CALORIES

450

TOTAL FAT

18g

TOTAL CARBS

48g

PROTEIN

13g

SANDWICHES & SNACKS

SMOOTHIES, SHAKES & DESSERTS

Carbs give you energy for any activity and for every body function. These recipes have significant carb levels—and they're also delicious! Whether you want something sweet or a little more tame, these smoothies, shakes, and desserts will satiate. You can enjoy them any time of the day, pairing them with meals or enjoying them on their own.

Inspired by the famous South Beach eatery of the same name, this creamy, fruity, and protein-packed smoothie is great for after a workout. In fact, the 3:1 ratio of carbs to protein is ideal for recovery. Add a scoop of protein powder to increase the protein by 20 to 30 grams.

BIG PINK SMOOTHIE

Makes 2 servings | Serving size 1 smoothie | Prep time 5 minutes | Cook time none

INGREDIENTS

1 cup frozen strawberries

1 cup frozen unsweetened raspberries

½ cup reduced-fat 2% Greek yogurt

1 cup coconut milk

2 tsp agave

DIRECTIONS

1 In a blender on high speed, blend all the ingredients and as many ice cubes as desired until smooth.

2 Pour the mixture into 2 chilled glasses and serve immediately.

NUTRITION FACTS

per serving

CALORIES

330

TOTAL FAT

8g

TOTAL CARBS

47g

PROTEIN

18g

ISLAND FRUIT SMOOTHIE

Makes 2 servings | **Serving size** 1 smoothie | **Prep time** 5 minutes | **Cook time** none

INGREDIENTS

1 orange, peeled and quartered

1 ripe banana, peeled and sliced

1 cup coconut water

1 cup frozen mango chunks

1 cup frozen pineapple chunks

DIRECTIONS

1 In a blender on high speed, blend all the ingredients and as many ice cubes as desired until smooth.

2 Pour the mixture into 2 chilled glasses and serve immediately.

This smoothie is my response to some of my athletes who have an affinity for sweeter fruit drinks. Combining tropical fruits into a smoothie might make you feel like you're on an island (minus the rum), but this is a great way to add carbs, vitamins, and antioxidants to your diet.

NUTRITION FACTS

per serving

CALORIES

250

TOTAL FAT

1 g

TOTAL CARBS

60 g

PROTEIN

2 g

CHANGE IT UP
You can replace the coconut water with fruit juice—but be mindful of changes to the nutritional information.

This recipe originated while taking the train into Manhattan for sparring sessions at the famed Gleason's Gym in Brooklyn. I'd take a juice made from carrot, apple, and ginger for the commute. And now you can take this colorful and nutritious juice with you anywhere.

NUTRITION FACTS

per serving

CALORIES

150

TOTAL FAT

0g

TOTAL CARBS

44g

PROTEIN

5g

SPICY CARROT JUICE

Makes 2 servings | **Serving size** 1 glass | **Prep time** 5 minutes | **Cook time** 1 minute

INGREDIENTS

½ head of cauliflower

8 carrots

2 golden beets, peeled

2 red-skinned apples, cored

½-inch (1.25cm) piece of fresh ginger

DIRECTIONS

1 In a pot on the stovetop over medium heat, cover the cauliflower with water. Bring to a boil and cook for 1 minute. Plunge the cauliflower into a bowl of ice water to stop the cooking process.

2 Cut all the ingredients to allow them to fit into the juicer chute. Place the carrots and beets in the juicer and process them before adding the cauliflower, apples, and ginger. Juice until only the pulp remains.

3 Pour the juice into 2 chilled glasses and serve immediately.

GREEN DETOX JUICE

Makes 1 serving | *Serving size* 1 glass | *Prep time* 5 to 10 minutes | *Cook time* none

INGREDIENTS

1 green apple, cored
3 celery stalks
1 cucumber
1 cup chopped kale

½ lemon, peeled
1-inch (2.5cm) piece of fresh ginger
1 sprig of mint

DIRECTIONS

1 Cut all the ingredients to allow them to fit into the juicer chute. Process all the ingredients until only the pulp remains.

2 Pour the juice to a chilled glass and serve immediately.

I dislike the word "detox" because your body is designed to detoxify your blood regularly and maintain homeostasis. That being said, *detox* is a buzzword that grabs attention. Now that I have yours, I can tell you that this nutritious juice is not only healthy but also refreshing and delicious.

NUTRITION FACTS

per serving

CALORIES

160

TOTAL FAT

0g

TOTAL CARBS

40g

PROTEIN

5g

Health and performance benefits of beets are quite astonishing according to all the research available on this amazing root vegetable. Beets are a fast-acting carbohydrate that relaxes smooth muscle tissue, like blood vessels, to speed up healing and recovery processes after workouts.

NUTRITION FACTS

per serving

CALORIES

250

TOTAL FAT

2 g

TOTAL CARBS

38 g

PROTEIN

22 g

BEET DOWN SHAKE

| Makes | 1 serving | Serving size | 1 shake | Prep time | 5 minutes | Cook time | none |

INGREDIENTS

4 whole tart dark cherries (fresh or frozen)

½ frozen banana

2 kale stalks, ribs removed and leaves chopped

½ cup unsweetened vanilla almond milk

½ cup raw organic beet juice

1 scoop vanilla protein powder

DIRECTIONS

1 In a blender on high speed, blend the cherries, banana, kale, and almond milk until smooth.

2 Add the juice and protein powder. Blend on high speed until smooth.

3 Pour the mixture into a chilled glass and serve immediately.

After intense workouts or long endurance sessions, I don't have much of an appetite, but I know I need to consume adequate energy—from protein and carbs—to help me recover. That's where this smoothie helps. This creamy and chocolatey giant is as much fun to make as it is to consume.

NUTRITION FACTS

per serving

CALORIES

600

TOTAL FAT

27g

TOTAL CARBS

52g

PROTEIN

47g

THE HEAVYWEIGHT

Makes 1 serving | **Serving size** 1 smoothie | **Prep time** 5 minutes | **Cook time** none

INGREDIENTS

2 tbsp all-natural peanut butter

½ cup quick or old-fashioned oats

1½ scoops chocolate protein

1 tbsp pure cocoa powder

1 cup 2% reduced-fat milk

DIRECTIONS

1 In a blender on high speed, blend all the ingredients and as many ice cubes as desired for 30 seconds to 1 minute.

2 Pour the mixture into a chilled glass and serve immediately.

PREP TIP *You can cut this recipe in half or in thirds if your energy needs aren't significant or if you've not had an active day.*

THE COUNSELOR

Makes 1 serving | *Serving size* 1 smoothie | *Prep time* 5 minutes | *Cook time* none

INGREDIENTS

1 cup coffee

1 frozen banana, cut into chunks

1 cup unsweetened vanilla almond milk

¼ cup old-fashioned oats

2 tbsp honey

1 tsp pure vanilla extract

DIRECTIONS

1 Pour the coffee into an ice cube tray and freeze overnight.

2 In a blender on high speed, blend the ice cubes, banana, almond milk, oats, honey, and vanilla until smooth.

3 Pour the mixture into a chilled glass and serve immediately.

I developed this recipe in honor of my lawyer, who loves coffee and is a consummate morning person. I'm a huge proponent of coffee— not only because of its caffeine content and ability to make you mentally alert, but because it's also an incredibly healthful drink for many ailments and conditions.

NUTRITION FACTS

per serving

CALORIES

270

TOTAL FAT

5g

TOTAL CARBS

55g

PROTEIN

4g

SMOOTHIES, SHAKES & DESSERTS

Matcha is a super-concentrated form of green tea. Because it's made from the whole ground leaf, you experience its full nutritional power. This recipe combines matcha's antioxidant benefits into a full meal of carbs, protein, and healthy fats for the perfect start to a day or a pre-workout snack.

NUTRITION FACTS

per serving

CALORIES

350

TOTAL FAT

12g

TOTAL CARBS

47g

PROTEIN

24g

MATCHA COOLER

| **Makes** 2 servings | **Serving size** 1 glass | **Prep time** 5 minutes | **Cook time** none |

INGREDIENTS

1½ frozen bananas

½ tbsp matcha powder

4 tbsp vanilla protein powder

½ tsp ground cinnamon

½ tsp ground cardamom

¼ tsp ground nutmeg

2 tbsp all-natural almond butter

1-inch (2.5cm) piece of fresh ginger

4 cups chopped baby spinach

2 cups unsweetened almond milk

1 tsp pure vanilla extract

DIRECTIONS

1 In a blender on high speed, blend all the ingredients until smooth.

2 Pour the mixture into 2 chilled glasses and serve immediately.

BLACK & BLUE SHAKE

Makes 2 servings | **Serving size** 1 shake | **Prep time** 5 minutes | **Cook time** none

INGREDIENTS

2 cups frozen blueberries

1 cup frozen broccoli

1 medium frozen banana

2 cups unsweetened vanilla almond milk

¼ cup vanilla protein powder

DIRECTIONS

1 In a blender on high speed, blend all the ingredients until smooth.

2 Pour the mixture into 2 chilled glasses and serve immediately.

I gave this recipe this name because of its color and its ability to make your immune system as strong as steel! This was one of the first smoothie formulations I ever made consistently, and it really helped me stay healthy during long training camps in the winter months of New York.

NUTRITION FACTS

per serving

CALORIES

330

TOTAL FAT

5g

TOTAL CARBS

40g

PROTEIN

34g

My brother Mike inspired this recipe, which was initially based on a joke. He loves spicy foods and said I should throw a jalapeño from the garden into a smoothie. We did it—and we liked it! The punch of the jalapeño is subdued by the creaminess of the avocado and the freshness of the mint.

MEAN GREEN JALAPEÑO SMOOTHIE

Makes	1 serving	Serving size	1 smoothie	Prep time	5 minutes	Cook time	none

INGREDIENTS

1 cup baby spinach

1 sprig of mint

¼ avocado

2 whole pitted dates

1 cup unsweetened coconut milk

1 tsp chopped jalapeño

½ tsp pure vanilla extract

dash of freshly squeezed lime juice

1 scoop vanilla protein powder

DIRECTIONS

1 In a blender on high speed, blend the spinach, mint, avocado, and dates until smooth.

2 Add the coconut milk in ¼ cup increments, continuing to blend on high speed until smooth.

3 Add the jalapeño in ¼ teaspoon increments, continuing to blend on high speed until smooth.

4 Add the vanilla, lime juice, protein powder, and as many ice cubes as desired. Continue to blend on high speed until smooth.

5 Pour the mixture into a chilled glass and serve immediately.

NUTRITION FACTS

per serving

CALORIES

350

TOTAL FAT

10 g

TOTAL CARBS

40 g

PROTEIN

25 g

SMOOTHIES, SHAKES & DESSERTS

PREP TIP // *Be careful with the amount of jalapeño you use because not all peppers have the same spiciness.*

I named this after the head strength and conditioning coach at Stony Brook University: George Greene. He serves this to the men's basketball team after each practice. I drink this nearly every single morning with black coffee or yerba mate. This delicious jolt gets me ready to attack the day!

GREENE MACHINE SMOOTHIE

Makes	1 serving		Serving size	1 smoothie		Prep time	5 minutes		Cook time	none

INGREDIENTS

½ cup chopped frozen broccoli

1½ cups baby spinach

fresh ginger

½ cup coconut water

½ cup unsweetened vanilla almond milk

1 scoop vanilla whey protein powder

1 tbsp chia seeds

DIRECTIONS

1 In a blender on high speed, blend the broccoli, spinach, and as much ginger as you desire until smooth.

2 Add the coconut water, almond milk, and protein powder. Blend on high speed until smooth.

3 Pour the mixture into a chilled glass, sprinkle the chia seeds over the top, and serve immediately.

NUTRITION FACTS

per serving

CALORIES

250

TOTAL FAT

5 g

TOTAL CARBS

20 g

PROTEIN

36 g

CHANGE IT UP

Add a medium avocado or 1 tablespoon of raw coconut oil for an added 120 calories.

FROZEN GREEK YOGURT

Makes *2 servings* | Serving size *1 cup* | Prep time *5 minutes* | Cook time *none*

INGREDIENTS

1 cup frozen berries (blueberries, raspberries, blackberries, etc.)

2 cups 2% low-fat Greek yogurt

2 tsp pure vanilla extract

2 tbsp honey

DIRECTIONS

1 In the bowl of a food processor, process all the ingredients until creamy, about 5 minutes.

2 Serve the frozen yogurt immediately or transfer it to an airtight container and freeze until ready to serve.

I don't personally have a sweet tooth, but I know many people do. Greek yogurt has a creamy mouthfeel that's similar to the consistency of home-churned ice cream. Sweetness from the fruit and honey gives anyone with a sweet tooth just what they need to quell any post-dinner cravings.

NUTRITION FACTS

per serving

CALORIES

225

TOTAL FAT

4 g

TOTAL CARBS

33 g

PROTEIN

17 g

SMOOTHIES, SHAKES & DESSERTS

CHANGE IT UP
Add nuts, granola, cereal, fruit, chocolate chips, whipped cream, fudge, or caramel.

I often find myself still hungry after dinner, but this is a perfect snack before bed. With tons of quality protein, a low-carb impact, and a good amount of satiating fats, this treat will turn your late night into something sweet, especially with added benefits from the chia seeds.

NUTRITION FACTS

per serving

CALORIES

200

TOTAL FAT

8g

TOTAL CARBS

10g

PROTEIN

24g

CHIA PROTEIN PUDDING

Makes	4 servings	Serving size	1 dish	Prep time	30 minutes	Cook time	none

INGREDIENTS

¼ cup vanilla protein powder

2½ cups unsweetened vanilla almond milk

¼ cup chia seeds

4 tbsp sliced almonds, divided

2 tsp ground cinnamon, divided

DIRECTIONS

1 In a bowl, whisk together the protein powder, almond milk, and chia seeds. Cover the bowl and refrigerate for 30 minutes or overnight to allow the mixture to thicken into a pudding.

2 Spoon an equal amount of pudding into 4 dessert dishes. Top each with 1 tablespoon of almonds and ½ teaspoon of cinnamon. Serve immediately or cover and refrigerate for up to 4 days.

RICE PUDDING

Makes 8 servings | *Serving size* 1 dish | *Prep time* 2 hours | *Cook time* 20 minutes

INGREDIENTS

8 cups 2% milk

1 cup uncooked long- or whole-grain rice

3 large eggs, yolks only, beaten

¾ cup granulated sugar

½ tsp pure vanilla extract

DIRECTIONS

1 In a pot on the stovetop over medium heat, combine the milk, rice, egg yolks, and sugar. Bring to a boil and cook until thickened and the rice is tender, about 20 to 25 minutes, stirring frequently.

2 Remove the rice mixture from the stovetop, stir in the vanilla, and allow to cool slightly.

3 Spoon an equal amount of pudding into 8 dessert dishes and chill for 2 to 3 hours before serving.

This pudding delivers a decent 11 grams of protein per serving, which is impressive for a dessert dish. Not only will you be able to enjoy a sweet treat any time during the day, but you'll also gain significant energy from the 50 grams of carbs per serving whenever you need a boost.

NUTRITION FACTS
per serving

CALORIES
300

TOTAL FAT
7 g

TOTAL CARBS
50 g

PROTEIN
11 g

SMOOTHIES, SHAKES & DESSERTS

INDEX

ABOUT THE AUTHOR

Chris Algieri is a professional boxer and kickboxer who held the World Boxing Organization (WBO) junior welterweight boxing title, the International Sport Karate Association (ISKA) world welterweight kickboxing title, and the World Kickboxing Association (WKA) world super welterweight kickboxing title during his more than 15-year professional career.

Chris has appeared on HBO, NBC, Showtime, Spike, and ESPN as a fighter and commentator. He's currently working toward another world boxing title to accomplish his goal of being a multiple-time world champion in two different sports.

Chris established himself as the "Pride of Huntington," fighting in Long Island, New York—just miles from his hometown of Greenlawn—at The Paramount in Huntington, selling out the venue nine consecutive times. In 2014, he defeated defending champion Ruslan Provodnikov for the WBO junior welterweight title—considered by *The Ring* magazine to be the upset of the year.

This victory led to the biggest fight of his life: In only his 21st professional boxing match, Chris moved up to the welterweight division to fight Manny Pacquiao for the WBO title. Although he lost that fight, he gained a lot of respect in going 12 rounds with the future Hall of Famer.

Outside the ring, Chris graduated from Stony Brook University with honors in May 2007 with a bachelor's of science in health care management and then went on to receive his master's degree from the New York Institute of Technology. He's certified as a sports nutritionist (CISSN) through the International Society of Sport Nutrition (ISSN).

Chris has worked closely with Stony Brook University as a consultant to the athletic department, helping develop a performance nutrition program for athletes and coaches. He has worked with nearly 500 Division I athletes from 16 different sport teams. He also speaks at various sports performance conferences and seminars.

ACKNOWLEDGMENTS

I'd like to thank Alpha Books and DK Publishing for choosing to work with me and helping me make a longtime goal of mine a reality. It's an honor to share my education, knowledge, and passion with so many. This has been a dream of mine all my life and the creation of this book has been in the works for more than four years.

Balancing a professional performance nutrition job for other athletes, launching my own professional boxing comeback, and simultaneously writing my first book were no easy tasks. I'd like to send a heartfelt thank you to Christopher Stolle, whose tireless efforts allowed this work to be completed, as well as to the designer, photographers, and recipe testers who made this something I can be proud of.

I'd like to thank my closest friends and family for always supporting me and giving me boundless positivity to power my efforts in all that I've set out to do in my life. I'd also like to thank Tony Ricci for guiding me on my performance nutrition journey from a young age.

Special thanks to my brother Mike and his wife Stephane, who have had to share the kitchen with me over the years while I created these recipes. Of course, the biggest thank you goes to my parents, Dominic and Adriana, for making this all possible in the first place. And lastly, to my grandparents, Carlos, Blanca, Santino, and Ann Marie, for instilling in me the importance of food, family, and culture.

PUBLISHER'S ACKNOWLEDGMENTS

The publisher wishes to thank Dana Angelo White (MS, RD, ATC) for creating the meal plans; Savannah Norris and Max Skillman for testing recipes; Casey No for assisting with food preparation and styling during the photo shoot; and Ryan Loco for his photographs of Chris.